Raising Capital and Borrowing Money

Everything You Wanted to Know About Raising Capital for the Start-Up Business, But Didn't Know Who or What to Ask...

By Marvin Morse, CPA

emerge publishing
TULSA, OKLAHOMA

21 20 19 18 17 7 6 5 4 3 2 1

RAISING CAPITAL AND BORROWING MONEY:
Everything You Wanted to Know About Raising Capital and Borrowing Money for the Startup Business but Didn't Know Who or What to Ask

emerge publishing
TULSA, OKLAHOMA

Published by:
Emerge Publishing, LLC
9521B Riverside Parkway, Suite 243
Tulsa, Oklahoma 74137
Phone: 888.407.4447
www.EmergePublishing.com

ISBN: 978-1-943127-69-6 Paperback
ISBN: 978-1-943127-70-2 Digital

BISAC Category:
BUS060000 BUSINESS & ECONOMICS / Small Business
BUS017030 BUSINESS & ECONOMICS / Corporate Finance / Venture Capital

Printed in the United States of America.

DEDICATION

I dedicate this book to all entrepreneurs who have struggled to secure the capital to launch their own business and to fulfill their dreams of business ownership. I congratulate those that were successful in accomplishing that considerable feat. For those that have failed to obtain funding, I offer my encouragement to continue trying, even though it may seem hopeless. One never knows when an unexpected event or new acquaintance can make it possible for us to achieve our goal.

I also dedicate it to my publisher, Christian Ophus, without whose insight and knowledge, this book, nor my first book, "The Little Book About Business Entity Selection", would have been possible.

Note to the Reader:

This book has been written for informational purposes only, and is intended to provide you general concepts concerning raising capital and borrowing money. It should not be solely relied upon for tax, legal or accounting advice. Every state is different, you should consult your own tax, legal and accounting advisers before engaging in any transaction.

CONTENTS

PREFACE

This book has been written after perhaps decades of thought. The author is founder of Morse & Co., a CPA firm based in Tulsa, OK, with clientele stretching to both coasts. He founded Morse & Co. after serving an international accounting firm for seven years. There is a crystal-clear reason he left the large firm and started a small, local CPA firm. He enjoyed working with small business owners and wanted to focus on that exclusively, and has done so continuously for more than thirty years. He continues to practice with Morse & Co. to the present time.

As you might imagine, the list of clients, types of industries, and personality types of hundreds of entrepreneurs has placed him in a very unique position to know how existing and prospective business owners think, their problems, and their concerns.

Many would-be entrepreneurs, if not most, never get past the task of obtaining capital to start their business. Of those that do overcome the initial hurdle of capital, the majority fail in their business due to the lack of adequate capital. It is clear that lack of capital is the number one cause of business failures and thus the prevention of business creation.

This book continues the adventures of Randy and Mike, which began in "The Little Book About Business Entity Selection", as they are challenged with capital and funding issues of their proposed ventures. Join them as they learn quickly to identify their start-up expenses and possible revenues. Learn from their struggles obtaining customers and clients. Witness their experiences with ending employment relationships, rapidly-changing family matters, and the realities of business issues that affect them. You will benefit much from their issues in accounting, billing, payroll, equipment leasing, banking, and other issues that are commonplace in the business world.

The highlights summary will also direct the reader to topical coverage of these particular items. However, it is recommended the entire book be read in that there are many little nuggets related to business start-up embedded in the narrative of each chapter that can't be covered in the summary.

SUMMARY

CHAPTER ONE:

Summarizes the process of forming a corporation or limited liability company online, obtaining a federal identification number on irs.gov., and opening of business bank accounts. The reader is reminded of the importance of an operating agreement for a limited liability company and articles of incorporation and bylaws for a corporation, as well as agreements for purchase and sale of ownership interests in the event of death or voluntary departure of a member or stockholder.

A non-technical, but very important, element of a business start-up is also introduced, and it is that of doubt. The element of doubt is sure to enter into the picture sooner or later for any new business venture.

CHAPTER TWO:

The sobering realization is that a new business requires cash. Many entrepreneurs will be intimidated by this realization and even more so by the fact they don't even know how much will be needed or how to find out.

Often times, bits and pieces of valuable information can be obtained from unsuspecting sources, such as from Freddy Simon, the restaurant owner. He let Randy and Mike know that they should expect to come up with most of the money and be totally at risk for their businesses. He also gave them ideas on the types of things they should be looking for such as equipment, supplies, insurance, and also to know how much cash they would need to manage these expenses until revenues were sufficient to cover them. At the same time, he offers a helping hand by offering to introduce them to a community bank president who deals with small business owners and just happens to be his daughter-in-law.

CHAPTER THREE

There are many sources of information related to business start-ups. This can be found on various websites. Local Chambers of Commerce have resources available to small business owners and some cities have small business incubator programs. It is a matter of dedicating the time to locate and study these multiple resources.

CHAPTER FOUR

Time is of the essence in many instances when contemplating a start-up. This could be due to seasonal demands, but in general, once a commitment is made to embark on a venture, the sooner it is begun the better. Just getting started is often the hardest part. It will appear to be a daunting task, with so many questions to be addressed and so much information to be assimilated.

CHAPTER FIVE:

A key ingredient for success, in a start-up involving partners, is that of an open dialogue between the partners as to the expectations of what each expects from the other. Although partnerships are difficult to maintain in business situations, a clear and concise agreement on the roles, obligations, and duties of each partner will provide the environment for a good partnership. Segregation of duties is the key. It is imperative this be agreed upon in the beginning, before the partnership is ever established. The partners must also be transparent and forthcoming about their financial resources and requirements. If these critical issues are not resolved up front, the partnership is likely a failure in the near future.

An equally crucial matter to resolve before even considering launching a business venture is the input and approval of a spouse or significant other. First, one will find their input valuable and helpful, bringing out ideas the proposed business owner has not considered. Second, without the complete support and endorsement of the venture on the part of the spouse or significant other, the venture will immediately have a huge first strike against itself.

CHAPTER SIX:

Often times, the spouse or significant other will support the new venture, but will be unable to provide much assistance due to their own business or professional endeavors. They will also not be willing to forego their own career to spend any significant time assisting with the new business. This must be accepted by the venturer.

It is extremely important to get started on cash flow projections for the start-up. Initially, it will seem futile, with more lines left blank than completed. Persistence is required here, because having blanks is actually providing a prompt for additional facts and knowledge. Like the age-old saying, "The harder you work, the luckier you get."

The ability to obtain mentoring from a seasoned veteran of the business world is one of the most fortunate relationships a prospective business founder can obtain. That individual can save countless hours and identify countless issues and problems, from which the individual can obviously benefit.

CHAPTER SEVEN:

Any individual who is seriously interested in starting a business should know what their cash requirements are, at least to a major degree, and be willing to research and make inquiries to confirm what they will need to purchase in the way of assets, as well as to identify the expenses they will incur. This is an absolute must, because it forms the minimum level of revenues that must be developed in order to survive. A practical way to do this is to prepare a monthly projection of cash flow for the first twelve months. It is also essential to list all expenses. Several expenses may not seem obvious to the untrained prospective business owner. This is where the combination of previous experience in the business, access to a mentor, and input from others such as accountants, insurance agents, and bankers is most beneficial. Finally, a factor for surprises of perhaps 10% should be added to the expense category. This provides a cushion for unexpected expenses. While these are unidentifiable, history suggests they will in fact occur.

Personal living expenses must also be identified and provided for.

At some point, the revenues must also be projected. At first this will cause great concern, because revenues are not certain as are expenses. So, unless an entrepreneur has a known customer or contract, this part can become very scary. But we all must begin somewhere. If one determines they do not have confidence as to revenue generation, they should likely abandon the idea of starting the business, at least for the time being.

It is also at this time that an inventory of capital sources must be itemized. This necessarily starts with those assets already available to the start-up proprietor. The obvious sources are savings, equity in homes, retirement accounts, credit cards and loans from family and friends. Each of these has their advantages and disadvantages of course.

Cash savings are the first to be used, as there are no tax or other factors of restraint. Credit cards are also easily used. The disadvantages of them are high rates of interest and immediate repayment terms, though relatively small in amount. The primary disadvantage of retirement accounts is the tax cost of accessing the funds, which include the regular tax rate and a 10% early-withdrawal penalty. For Simple IRA accounts the penalty is 25% if the plan has not been established for two years. So, it easy to see that the total tax cost of federal tax, federal penalties, and state tax can easily reach a minimum of 30%.

Loans from family and friends might have the advantage of relatively low interest rates and flexible repayment terms. The very threatening disadvantage is that in the event such loans could not be repaid, family relationships could become tense or even adversarial, and lifetime friendships could be destroyed. One of the story characters was given the idea of borrowing from a family member, but holding the retirement account in reserve as a last-ditch opportunity to pay the family member if the business failed.

Options of home equity include a complete refinancing of the home, or securing a home equity line of credit. A word of caution on this one is that mortgage lenders often are skeptical about lending to new business owners. This option might be best executed prior to leaving one's employment.

The decisions regarding capital formation will be different for everyone, but one thing is certain. The assumption that an "angel" will step in from out of the blue to write a check for all your business funding is a faulty one, and one that just isn't going to happen, except perhaps in the rarest of circumstances.

The person seriously contemplating a start-up will soon desire to spend all their time on it. This includes not only identifying the start-up costs, but also the securing of business through whatever means they can. Should one find themselves unwilling to do this for fear of losing the security of employment, they are not ready for the risk and should abandon the idea immediately. The person who is not willing to abandon the effort will have to make a hard decision to leave their employment at some point, and that point will be before all uncertainties as to success have been resolved.

One thing in favor of the entrepreneur is that most people love to help someone who is struggling to start their business.

It is clear that doubt and fear will be present during the start-up period. This is a good thing in that it keeps us alert and cautious. We must remember that even a business that has gained good profitability can fail. So, a certain degree of fear and humility is a healthy situation.

Two of the most misunderstood expense items for a business with employees are insurance and payroll taxes. The common types of insurance are fire and casualty, liability, and workers' compensation.

In addition to the above, there could be other insurance requirements that are peculiar to a particular industry. One example is that of performance bonds for those in construction contracting.

Payroll taxes are complicated even for seasoned business owners. That is why many small business owners utilize the services of a payroll service provider to be certain all requirements are met. The penalties for late payment are substantial.

Nevertheless, a business owner should understand how the payroll tax is structured. It consists of withholding requirements for each employee for federal income tax, social security tax, Medicare tax, and state income tax. These are withheld from employees' wages and must be remitted to the government agencies at frequent intervals, along with matching contributions of social security and Medicare taxes. Thus, the employee pays 7.65% and is matched by the employer for the same amount. This is often within three days of payment of payroll, but as infrequent as monthly for very small employers. State withholding is paid monthly in most states. Federal payments must be done electronically for all but the smallest businesses. Many states also require monthly payments. The employer must also pay federal and state unemployment taxes. These are the sole burden of the employer. State unemployment taxes are paid quarterly with a report that calculates the amount owed. The rate is set by the state, based on unemployment claims filed on the business. There is a minimum for new business. There is also a ceiling on the amount of wages for which the tax must be paid. The federal unemployment tax is much less than the state. It must be paid quarterly if the liability exceeds $100. Otherwise it can be paid with the annual report due January 31 of each year. The federal rate is .7% of the first $7,000.

It is little wonder that some small business owners avoid the complications of payroll taxes by treating their employees as independent contractors. However, this is a very dangerous route to take. Internal Revenue Service aggressively polices such activities, and has adopted severe penalties for the practice of treating employees as independent contractors. There is further risk from disgruntled former employees who might claim they were an employee. This person will owe much more in tax than expected due to the fact they are liable for the full 15.3% employment tax. There is further exposure with state employment commissions if a terminated former employee files for unemployment with them. This could lead to a minimum three-year exposure to state and federal unemployment taxes, plus penalties and interest. This is a shipwreck one can't afford to risk.

The owner of a business with no employees must include the social security and Medicare tax in their quarterly estimate payments, along with their estimated income tax. The quarterly estimates are due April 15, June 15, September 15, and January 15.

After learning of the many issues related to insurance and employment taxes, it is clear that a new business owner must make arrangements to affiliate with an insurance professional and a certified public accountant. Both of these should be carefully chosen for their expertise in working with start-up operations and that are familiar with the industry in which one operates.

CHAPTER EIGHT:

It is quite amazing that one single event can often provide the motivation to move ahead with a venture. One customer or project can be the deciding factor that pushes the hopeful entrepreneur over the edge, supplying just enough confidence at the precise moment for them to move ahead.

In any event, it is true that all the good planning, accounting, expense management, and technical expertise means nothing if there are no customers and thus no revenue. Sales and marketing has to be top of mind at all times.

CHAPTER NINE:

Life becomes complicated and hectic when a firm decision is made to start the business of one's dreams. It is great to identify problems and issues and to talk about them; however, it is often easier said than done. The solving of one issue often unveils yet another issue to be addressed.

One of the most traumatic events of this process is that of revealing your plans to your present employer. This is, in most cases, unpleasant if not tense. However, once in a great while, something good will happen, and that something will assist the aspiring business owner in profitable ways.

Financing and leasing options will have to be pursued and understood to acquire assets. The professionals described earlier have to be sought out. Prospective customers need to be called on and details secured. Timing commitments and billing rates must be addressed. Don't be surprised if customers negotiate discounted rates, knowing how desperately you need the business.

CHAPTER TEN:

This chapter continues to address the minute details that the entrepreneur must resolve. It also demonstrates the value of business referrals from those whom the proposed customer or client trusts. The benefits of having prior experience with issues of potential clients is also stressed. Finally, the super-critical aspects of marketing are continued.

CHAPTER ELEVEN:

The drama associated with a business start-up is no better demonstrated than by the irate employer when they learn of the planned departure to become a competitor. The expected outcome is negative at best, but occasionally it can become downright ugly. A shrewd entrepreneur will be prepared for this and use it to reinforce their determination to succeed. After all, we cannot control the actions and thoughts of others.

If a start-up is in need of accounting services, they will learn that a CPA firm can't provide both accounting services and certain types of financial statement preparation services. This is dictated by their code of professional ethics, which applies to all certified public accountants. Depending on the type service chosen for the CPA firm, they can usually assist in locating a firm for the second service.

CHAPTER TWELVE:

The insurance needs, including mandatory coverage, of a commercial enterprise can be quite daunting for the previously uninformed. Equipment, including vehicles must be insured against theft and loss due to fire and casualty. While this coverage is probably mandatory from a pure business perspective, it can be required as part of the terms of a leasing or financing agreement. Liability insurance protects the business in the event of an accident resulting in damages to a third-party caused by the acts of the business, including its employees. Again, good business practice would warrant this coverage, but many customers might also require it in order to secure their business. Workers' compensation is mandatory under state law to provide medical and disability insurance for employees injured on the job. All states provide a workers' compensation fund for employers who can't obtain affordable coverage from standard insurance carriers. Business owners can opt out of workers' compensation, which many do, especially if they have medical coverage otherwise.

It is important to work with an insurance person who is familiar with the industry and who has access to all the types of insurance required. For many business owners, this will be what is referred to a general agent, who works with numerous insurance companies. For those types of entities who require bonding, it is crucial that the agent work with providers of these performance bonds. An agent experienced in the industry will also be familiar with problems and pitfalls of those in the industry and can provide valuable insight for business operations, such as cash management, as well as bidding and pricing. They may have live examples of the casualties resulting from failure to employ these good practices and procedures.

Insurance premiums may be able to be financed through a premium finance agreement, with a sizeable down-payment.

Finally, the insurance professional may be able to give good referrals, due to their contacts in the industry.

Some are surprised when lessors and banks require personal guaranties of all owners, and spouses, of small business organizations seeking credit. This is standard policy and financing will not be accomplished if the owners are unwilling to provide the guaranties.

Finally, the practical results of marketing and personal requests for work are shown to be fruitful.

CHAPTER THIRTEEN:

Again, it is helpful to have access to an experienced mentor in the start-up phase. They have the experience to point out obvious omissions of expenses in cash projections and to note errors in expenses that are provided. Some omissions may even indicate a process or procedure has not been addressed because the cost of it is not itemized. The ability to identify these prior to sharing the projection with a potential lender, such as a bank, will avoid embarrassment and enhance the chances of obtaining the financing, because it fosters confidence in the entrepreneur on the part of the banker.

Expect delays when planning the start-up. Lack of funding on the client or customer's part is one good example. It is important to plan for these and to not let them cause despair.

CHAPTER FOURTEEN:

Even when outsourcing payroll and payroll tax, there are still details that must be addressed. For example, just to get it set up, the payroll service company will need W-4 forms for each employee in order to determine income tax withholding. In addition, any departments or special coding for payroll will need to be set up. Decisions will have to be made regarding which day payroll will end and which day checks will be released. If the business needs to track payroll by job, such as those in the construction contracting business, procedures will have to be developed for coding payroll by job. The logistics of delivery or pick-up of the actual checks will have to be determined. If direct deposit is to be utilized, then bank information for each employee will have to be provided.

Even though the payroll provider uses their own checks, the new business will need checks for other expenditures. These will have to comply with software, such as QuickBooks if the checks are to be printed using the software. If not, then any type of check suitable for the business may be used.

The accounting for any business engaged in contracting is more complicated than normal, due to the need to accumulate costs by job. Software that will accommodate this type of accounting is a must for this type business. Most direct costs will be coded to the appropriate expense category, but also must be coded to a job number. To further complicate matters, some expenses may apply to multiple jobs and some expenses of the same type might relate to non-contract work, many times referred to as service work. It becomes quickly apparent that the services of an accountant versed in these matters is desirable.

Be careful in the start-up phase that funds you have deposited in your bank account are actually collected by your bank and can be used to cover checks that need to be written, or for which a cashiers' check is needed. Many, if not all, banks place a hold on deposits until they are cleared and the bank is assured they will collect the funds.

Leasing is a viable financing option for a start-up in some instances. There are two types of leases. First is the regular operating lease, which allows the lessee to pay a certain amount for a given number of months to use the equipment. They are typically given the option to return the equipment at the end of the lease term or to purchase it at its fair market value. The second option is the capital, or financing, lease. Under the capital lease, the lessee owns the equipment at the end of the term. A down-payment that varies with the financial capabilities and credit history of the lessee may be required. This lease is recorded the same as a purchase, with the asset and lease liability recorded on the books of the lessee; whereas, the operating lease payments are charged to rent expense as paid.

There are many details associated with the start-up of a business. In addition to those noted above, matters such as vehicle purchases, PO boxes, storage facilities, and others come into play along with putting finishing touches on the cash flow projections as these events unfold.

CHAPTER FIFTEEN:

The entrepreneur will definitely want to develop a relationship with a good, small business banker immediately. There are two distinct advantages to this. First of all, banking services will be needed for such items as credit card services, online banking, etc. Second, it is good to get to know the banker as soon as possible to provide exposure to the business owner. While the bank may not lend any funds to the new business in the very early stages, it is imperative that a track record be established. There will likely come a time where a loan will be needed badly. They may even be able to help in the initial stages with a home equity loan or vehicle loan. The sooner one can start gaining credibility the better. It is highly recommended the bank be one with a proven record of small business lending and one who is a major SBA lender. Of course, SBA stands for Small Business Administration, a branch of the federal government that guarantees up to 90% of approved small business loans. It is not always the case, but as a general rule, a smaller community bank as opposed to a branch of a national bank is better suited for the start-up.

A good small business bank can help in other ways, other than lending. They can provide business advice on avoiding pitfalls and also marketing techniques in some cases, depending upon the business involved. In addition to the standard advice of conservative spending and cash management, the development of recurring revenue streams is a good example of some of the advice that might be available.

Insurance needs for service businesses are normally simple and affordable, unless professional liability insurance is required. It is still advisable to seek out a reputable general agent who has knowledge in the industry of the aspiring business owner. They can offer health and disability insurance in addition to the standard fire and casualty and general liability insurance. Again, since they are likely seasoned in their business, they will have business experience that might be shared, along with marketing ideas. They also may be willing to share referrals with their customer, especially once they have grown to know and trust them.

A potential marketing idea for someone in the service business is to join a business referral organization, sometimes referred to as a tips club. This is particularly true for one in a service business with wide appeal to both individuals and businesses.

CHAPTER SIXTEEN:

It can't be emphasized enough the importance of accuracy in cash flow projections. Mistakes are easily made when dealing with expenses one is not familiar with, such as the various tax expenses. A good mentor in this area is essential.

Most entrepreneurs are surprised by the work that starts to come to their attention once they have made an all-out commitment to the business. It is getting past the initial fear and doubt that is the most difficult. Existing contacts from experience in the industry is the most valuable. These contacts already know you and are more willing to give you an opportunity than someone you never met. Although, that is not to say business cannot be obtained from complete strangers. If contacts are with public institutions, such as state, local, and city government, the new business owner will still have to compete through bidding processes, but at least the contact will allow them to get a foot in the door.

Accurate financial statements may be required to obtain certain work as well. Some customers may require financial ratios that are positive, such as the current ratio and debt-to-equity. This may be a struggle that the start-up must address in order to obtain the business, even though the customer believes they have the ability to do quality work. A current ratio of 1:1 may be required. This indicates that liabilities due within one yard are no greater than cash and other assets that will be converted to cash within one year, such as accounts receivable and inventory. The existence of at least some small amount of earnings in the current year is also highly desirable, as is an appropriate level of capital versus all debt, even if all the debt isn't due within one year.

As business does begin to become available, it is important to make sure resources are available to do the work timely. Nothing is worse than to accept work and then not complete it timely and with high quality. It would be better to not accept the work than to accept it and then do a poor job. Long-term credibility is very important. This includes the ability to secure any specialized equipment needed for the new work.

CHAPTER SEVENTEEN:

Most new business owners will have some individuals who will go out of their way to refer business to them. These may or not be close friends. It may very well be just an acquaintance. These individuals just find gratification in helping the struggling entrepreneurs, and may not even be a business owner themselves. Needless to say, their help should be accepted with humility and gratitude, and follow-up with their referrals should be handled quickly and efficiently.

The establishment of a relationship with a community banker who specializes in lending to small business, and that is knowledgeable with Small Business Administration lending, has previously been mentioned. However, it is time well spent to learn a little about how bankers operate and their constraints. Many business owners do not realize that all banks are highly regulated by federal or state agencies, depending on whether they are a federal or state chartered bank. The regulators scrutinize all loans made by the bank, and classify those which might seem marginal. Classifying a loan basically means the bank has to set up a loss reserve for the loan, which in turn causes a reduction in the bank's capital. This reduces the loans the bank can make and thus impacts their earning capability. This is one reason banks are cautious when considering a loan to a start-up. Even if they were inclined to take a calculated risk and make the loan, they know they will suffer at the hands of the regulators in a very short timeframe.

Bankers evaluate each loan opportunity using a term called the three C's. The three items are character, capacity, and collateral. They must first determine if the proposed borrower is of good character. Understandably, they don't want to make a loan to someone of poor character, as that individual might not really want to repay the loan, particularly if the business did not do well. Capacity represents the ability to repay the loan from earnings of the business. This deals with existing, or reasonably expected, cash flow. Collateral is the last, and it is likely the least important of the three. Collateral is intended to provide a margin of safety, but the truth of the matter is that no banker wants to rely on the collateral to repay the loan. As expected, the would-be business owner is often lacking in proven capacity and perhaps collateral, even though they may pass the character test with flying colors.

Banks are able to extend a variety of loans. For example, a business may have a peak season and a slow season. It may need to borrow to meet expenses during the slow season and pay the loan back during its peak season. The bank can extend a line of credit that meets that need. It is granted during the slow season and expects repayment during the peak. Equipment loans are used to finance new equipment and are normally amortized over three to five years, with monthly payments that include interest.

CHAPTER EIGHTEEN:

The harder one works, the luckier they get is an old saying, but one that is so true. The more effort and attention given to any situation the more the situation improves. This includes marketing for the new business. The results will often be unexpected by the business owner, maybe even unbelievable.

The proper launching of a new business not only requires a supreme effort on the part of the entrepreneur, but also a lot of help from friends, family, business acquaintances, mentors, bankers, insurance professional, and certified public accountants. Although the driving force of the start-up has to come from the entrepreneur, the support and advice of these other individuals will prove to be priceless.

CHAPTER NINETEEN:

New challenges will be constantly facing the growing business. Capital and financing requirements become regular and increasingly more difficult. The difficulties of the initial start-up are significant; however, there is never a time in the life of a business that all is perfect, at least for many, many years. The business owner must be constantly looking and planning ahead to be prepared for the coming events. There will be hostile competitors that strain profit margins. There will be risks of taking on new projects that require new equipment and perhaps new skills. Needs for services and employees change and evolve quickly. Profitability and cash flow must be monitored at all times.

LIFE IS NEVER DULL AT THE HELM OF
A NEW BUSINESS!

CHARACTERS

Randy	Aspiring lawn, landscape, and construction company owner. He eventually names his business First Premier Lawn and Landscaping, Inc.
Mike	Aspiring self-employed information technology consultant. He eventually names his business Horizons IT Consultants, LLC.
Vicky	Randy's spouse and career medical professional.
Heather	Mike's spouse, homemaker, and accountant.
Josh	Randy's partner, who is not versed in business matters, but is a good operations person. He has two nice customers who agreed to do business with Josh and Randy. His Father has also

offered to lend the new business up to $50,000 if needed.

Harry Hanson Semi-retired CPA who counsels Randy and Mike on various issues related to starting their businesses. He had previously instructed them on business entity selection in "Everything You Wanted to Know About Business Entity Selection." Mike and Randy met him through Liz.

Liz College friend of Mike, and owner of a successful construction company specializing in school buildings. She refers Randy and Mike to Harry Hanson through her CPA.

Freddy Simon Owner of Freddy's Barbecue and long-time acquaintance of Randy and Mike, who offers sage advice on starting a business to them. Also, father-in-law of a local banker, to whom he refers Randy and Mike.

Sharlene Ellis Daughter-in-law of Freddy Simon and president of Regency Bank, a prominent local community bank and small business lender. Shari, as she preferred to be called, helps Randy and Mike in several matters.

Norman Manager of Java Don's coffee house and friend of Randy, who he encourages and refers other customers to.

Tim Mike's boss at work, who actually helps Mike with his business in unexpected ways.

Travis Equipment dealer who helps Randy locate initial equipment for his business and helps him even further by securing a lessor, allowing Randy to come up with less capital. He even takes a big risk by purchasing the equipment before Randy has any money for a down-payment.

Ruthie Friend of Liz and upscale restaurant owner. Liz introduces Mike to Ruthie, who becomes his first client.

Morton & Co. Local CPA firm for which Heather had formally worked. She returns to work there part-time and is involved with assisting Randy establish his accounting procedures and doing his daily accounting.

Morton & Co. assist both Mike and Randy with business referrals.

Ted Randy's former boss. He becomes very angry when Randy announces his plans to start a business, terminating Randy right at that moment. He later would plague Randy with competitive bidding on work for the City.

Steve Palmer General insurance agent who assists both Randy and Mike with their respective insurance

	needs. Steve also offers business strategy and business development leads for them.
Paul Burnhart	Director of Parks for the City. He encourages Randy and ultimately helps him obtain bidding opportunities with the City which leads to several projects.
Don Adams	Randy's first new customer, which was for lawn services. Don eventually refers two even larger customers to Randy.

CHAPTER ONE

DOUBT CREEPS IN

Mike fumbled for the alarm as he was rudely awakened from a deep sleep. It was 5:00am and he had promised himself that he would arise early to work on setting up his new limited liability company It had been two weeks since Randy and he had visited with Harry Hanson. Between family activities and a week-long trip for an out-of-town project with a client of his firm, the time had just plain vanished. He planned to form the LLC and secure his federal identification number this morning before he went to the office.

He was convinced he needed just a single member LLC that would take the default status as a disregarded entity, allowing him to simply report his business income and expenses on Schedule C in his personal return. Thankfully, Harry had shown him this was his easiest and most economical way to go when Randy and he had met with Harry two weeks ago, which now seemed like the distant past.

Mike poured a cup of hot coffee as he sat down at his laptop. He soon was on the Secretary of State website and found the format easy to follow. He entered the name he had chosen for his company, Horizons IT Consultants, LLC. He soon had entered his credit card information and was done with the formation.

The IRS webpage, irs.gov., was also easy to navigate and he had obtained the federal ID number in just a few minutes, remembering to check the box stating the ID was needed for banking purposes only, which would hopefully let IRS know not to expect a separate tax return for his business. He also told IRS he did not expect to have any employees, which also would put them on notice that his business would have no payroll reports to file. Mike was relieved at the thought of having no employees and no payroll to meet. The real truth was, he admitted to himself, that **doubt was beginning to creep in** as to whether he could even generate enough revenue for his own family's needs. His wife was not working due to needing to be home with their two young kids.

At any rate, he could now open his business account if he could come up with any funds to open it with. He had just a small amount of savings and that was it. As he headed for the shower, he wondered if he had made a mistake thinking he could pull off this idea of owning his own firm.

Mike made a note in his phone to talk to the lawyer in his building about an operating agreement for his single-member LLC, although he had found some examples on various websites. However, he remembered Harry's comments about that and concluded it might be wise to ask a lawyer to do it instead.

He had not even touched base with Randy and would like to hear how he was doing on his new venture. Maybe they could have lunch one day this week.

Randy had been busy since Mike and he had met with Harry Hanson in Fayetteville two weeks earlier. He laughed to himself as he recalled attempting to explain all he had learned about business entities from the meeting with Harry to his partner. His partner had stared into space as Randy went meticulously through it all. When Randy said, he thought they should form a corporation and be taxed as a C Corp. initially, his partner had exclaimed immediately, "I could not agree more. Let's get it done!"

He had not had an issue forming the corporation on the Secretary of State website, breezing through the whole process in fifteen minutes. The hard part was coming up with a name, which his partner and he finally agreed would be First Premier Lawn and Landscape, Inc. He was still amazed that the cost to form a corporation in his state was only $50. He also found irs.gov easy to navigate and easily obtained the federal identification. He stated that the reason for obtaining the number was forming a new business and told IRS he expected to have four employees. He guessed that would trigger IRS to expect the new entity to file not only income tax returns but something to do with payroll also. He admitted that he did not even know what he did not know when it came to payroll and that he would need a lot of help with that. He also suffered a **twinge of doubt** as to whether he could actually manage the business to meet payroll. But his partner was confident he could round up enough work to keep himself and two employees busy most of the time, and Randy himself would be the fourth employee. Randy grimaced as he quickly thought of the equipment that would be required for the new business. He was also **having some doubt** about whether he could find a way to finance that and manage to meet other expenses that were sure to arise.

Opening the bank account was a breeze. His partner and he each came up with $1,000 of capital to fund the new account. That was largely consumed by the legal fees for preparing articles of incorporation and bylaws, not to speak of the agreement between his partner and him regarding the value to be used and method of payment and interest in the event one of them chose to depart from the business or died. They agreed that nothing would be paid the first year and they would adjust the value annually after that when the corporation filed its income tax returns. They realized this to be a risky endeavor, due to the possibility of them failing to update the value, but the use of a formula based on a multiple of average annual earnings could not be used the first couple years anyway.

Randy was suddenly jolted from his deep thoughts by a limb crashing to the ground beside him that his helper had just trimmed from the tree he was standing beside. He really needed to start paying attention, but just couldn't stop thinking about this new venture.

Just as Randy was finishing the tree-trimming project, his cell phone rang from inside his truck. He was able to reach it in time to answer and find Mike on the phone. Mike was wanting to catch up and wondered if Randy had time for lunch the next day at their favorite barbecue spot, Freddy's Barbecue, which was run by an old friend of theirs. They agreed to meet there the following day.

Neither of them had even the remotest idea of what lay ahead. Had they known the thrills, hurdles, and doubt facing them in the weeks ahead, they may have very well cancelled that lunch meeting.

CHAPTER TWO

MONEY, REALLY?

Randy and Mike arrived at Freddy's about the same time, greeting the owner, Freddy Simon as they found a table near the back so they could talk. They recounted what they had accomplished the past two weeks and arrived at the same conclusion. It had been great learning all about the best entity and all the tax ramifications for a new business, but they now realized that was only the first minor, and probably the easiest, step to take. They now were facing the reality and magnitude of the capital needed to do this, and they both confessed their periods of doubt. Yes, they now fully acknowledged they really would need money. And perhaps a lot of it.

Just about that time, Freddy came over to say hello to them, and see what they had been doing. "Freddy," Mike volunteered, "we have been working on starting our own business", and offered him a quick background on the events of the past few weeks. "But to be honest, Freddy, we are getting cold feet because we aren't sure we can come up with the capital we need to do it."

"Well, how much capital do you need?" Freddy asked. Freddy had actually opened his restaurant many years ago, after working for several different restaurants in the city. Randy and Mike clearly had not determined how much capital they needed, and Randy replied, "We honestly don't know."

Freddy did not seem too surprised, and continued quickly. "Then you shouldn't give up on it before you even know how much it is. Tell you what I will do. My daughter-in-law is a banker, and she works a lot with small business owners down at Regency Bank. They are a community bank, and she even knows how to help people get funding help from the government. I think she calls it SBA loans. Anyway, you should give her a call and see if she can help you. She is a nice person, but also very honest. I am sure she will tell you if you are barking up a tree. I will give you her name and number when you leave. But in the meanwhile, I suggest you start figuring out how much money you will need for equipment, supplies, insurance, and all those things. And don't forget to compute what you need to cover the overhead until the money starts coming in. Otherwise, you might go broke before you get going good. And one more thing, no one is going to lend you money unless you have put all the money you can get into your business. They want you to have as much, or even more, to lose as they do. And they don't want it to be easy for you to give up, because there will be difficult times ahead," Freddy concluded as he rushed off to help out a customer.

Randy and Mike were speechless as they finished their lunch and prepared to get back to work. They never dreamed Freddy could tell them so much so quickly, but then again, he had managed to start and run a restaurant for over thirty years. They knew their work was laid out for them, and wished they had Harry, or someone, to turn to for help even before they went to see Freddy's daughter-in-law. Did they dare contact Harry again? Would Liz take time from her busy schedule to help them get started in the right direction? Liz, Mike's friend from college, and now a successful construction company owner, had introduced them to Harry, but Mike did not think it proper to contact Harry direct, unless Liz gave the okay to the idea. The two were at a loss and dropped into silence for a while.

Mike broke their silence by saying, "It would be a little presumptive to contact Harry again without Liz's approval. I even hate to bother her, because she has her hands full with her own business".

Randy waited a moment and then replied, "Well which will embarrass you the least, calling Liz or looking like a complete dummy when we go see Freddy's daughter-in-law?" "Calling Liz" was Mike's short answer. "I can just see if she has someone she knows that can help us out," he continued on.

"I will see what I can find on the internet," Randy volunteered, "since you are going to talk to Liz." Their excitement level was a quantum leap below what it had been only two weeks ago.

CHAPTER THREE

NITTY-GRITTY DETAILS

Mike frowned mentally as he left Randy, just thinking about bugging Liz again. He wouldn't blame her if she told him to take a hike. After all, he hadn't kept in touch for years, and now he was calling every two weeks asking for a favor. Maybe he could offer to do something for her, but then again, what would it be? He decided to send an email first, thinking that would give her an easy out if she didn't want to deal with him. He composed the email as soon as he was back at his desk and hit send, hoping for the best. He immediately got Liz's auto-reply saying she was out until Thursday and to call her cell phone if it were urgent. Of course, Mike wasn't about to do that.

Randy returned to the landscaping project he was supervising at the City-County Library, a big job he had helped bid and present to the Board of County Commissioners. He felt confident he knew the landscape and lawn care business inside out and backwards, but was feeling uncertain about his knowledge and ability to start one of his own. Yet, he was determined and couldn't wait to get home that evening to start his research.

Randy got a text from Mike saying Liz was out until Thursday, but in the meantime, he had remembered seeing something from the Chamber of Commerce about its small business division and decided that he would investigate that.

That evening Randy spent several hours reading information available from various websites regarding business start-ups. He became particularly interested in one that provided some insight into the need for a business plan. He learned that he should be in a position to formalize his plans, including the equipment he would need to start his business and the personnel he would need to do the business. Not only that, he should be able to equate this to dollars, or capital, as it was often referred to. He also read a great deal about the "hidden costs" of a business operation such as insurance and various taxes. The perils of inadequate cash management also seemed to appear again and again.

At 12:30 A.M, Randy realized several things. One of them was that he needed to meet with his partner and reduce to writing exactly what business they could expect to generate initially and the equipment and personnel they would need and what it would cost. He also began to realize that he had a lot of work to do determining what expenses would be mandatory and how long would they incur expenses before the money started coming in. Randy also understood that a lot of the business he knew was available might require a bond, and he didn't even know if he could secure a bond. Thoughts of advertising, vehicle costs, and supplies raced through his mind until he realized one final thing - he was exhausted and needed to get some rest unless he was going to be worthless the following day.

Mike had slept restlessly during the night, as he lay awake thinking of Freddy's comments regarding the difficulties of securing credit or capital for a business start-up. Freddy's comments about knowing what he would require for expenses and having more to lose than a lender or investor haunted him as he tossed and turned through the night. He realized that he did not have huge capital needs to start his business, since his was a service business. Sure, he might need a few thousand dollars for computers and a server, but nothing serious. His biggest problem was supporting his family until the business could produce adequate revenues. He knew that he was capable of operating an IT service business, at least from a technical standpoint, but he had little experience in new client development. He did know a few business owners that might consider hiring him for their IT needs, but nothing was certain at this point. At the same time, he knew his industry was growing because his company was constantly assigning him to new clients. But how was he to tap into that pipeline, and how long would it take? Could he last long enough? Freddy had been right on the money with that comment.

Mike arose at 5:00, since he was not sleeping well anyway. He logged on to his laptop and went to the Chamber of Commerce website. He quickly learned that they did have a small business council, designed to help small business owners, including a referral list of outside resources.

He also learned from a quick web search that the Small Business Administration had various loan programs designed to help small businesses and that they also provided financial support to an organization called Service Corps of Retired Executives, or S.C.O.R.E. This organization apparently offers assistance with various business issues provided by experienced current and former business people. Mike wondered if they could assist Randy and him with their capital needs.

Through the night, both Randy and Mike had come to realize in their own way that they were faced with some **very crucial nitty-gritty details** regarding their future business prospects.

CHAPTER FOUR

THE RACE IS ON!

Randy groaned as he turned off his alarm at 6:00 A.M. It had been a fitful night, and he did not feel at all like rushing to the job site to meet the concrete supplier at 7:00. He quickly showered and slipped out of the house without waking his wife. Feeling groggy still, he stopped at Java Don's for a strong cup of coffee. Soon he was feeling alert and thoughts were whirling in his head. He knew **the race was on for him in a big-time way**. The peak season for his type of business was soon approaching and if he was to launch it this year, it would have to be very soon. He began to think of all the things he knew had to be done, and wondered how many more had not even occurred to him. Realizing the library job would be wrapping up the following day and that nothing big was on tap for the following week, he decided he would ask the owner of his company if he could take a few days off, maybe even starting tomorrow. After all, he had worked some long hours bringing this job in on time and hadn't taken a day off all year. Surely his boss would be sympathetic. He sent a text to his hopeful partner, letting him know they had to meet after work to get down to some serious planning. The driver of the concrete truck called to say he was running fifteen minutes late, giving Randy time to finish his coffee and do some more thinking.

The things he knew were, that his partner had very good relations with two large, local property management owners that would refer jobs to them. Randy also knew himself to be fairly well known and respected in the business around town. He reasoned he could obtain a fair number of jobs if he had the ability to get them done - a big if at this point. He also felt the time was right to enter the lawn maintenance business as the premier company doing that had just lost their founder and president due to retirement. A competitive position in this area would surely bring new business. Randy felt some guilt at the thought of competing with his present company and purposed not to solicit any of their potential business until after his departure from their employ. Then, all bets were off, and the most competitive team would surely benefit from the work. He actually thought there was plenty of work to go around, as his company sometimes had to turn work away.

The things Randy didn't know related to the exact make and models of equipment they would have to purchase, how much it would cost, and how to pay for it. He also didn't know how much money he would need to get started, and to be truthful, exactly how to estimate it all in a way that would make sense. Maybe Liz or Harry could help Mike and he get organized on this stuff, he optimistically thought as he realized he would now be late meeting the concrete driver.

Mike's day had started on a bad note. Not only had he not slept well and had arisen early, he really hadn't found all that much to help him from the research he had done. He was beginning to feel pressure to get something done or abandon the whole idea. At the rate he was going, it surely wouldn't be long before his work would suffer, not to mention his family life. As he said goodbye to his wife and two children, he made a promise to himself that he would make a decision by the end of the week, one way or the other.

On the drive to work, Mike roughly figured that he could make it for only three months with his savings and family budget, and that didn't even address health insurance. He had not talked too much with his wife yet, but knew he had to sit down and go through this with her. She had been supportive of the idea when they discussed it in the past, but they had not drilled down into the finances, or lack thereof, of starting a business from scratch. One good thing was that she had a minor in accounting from South Central State and had worked part-time at an accounting office for about a year. She could hopefully help him with that part of the business.

Mike was totally surprised to find Liz's email when he arrived at work. She was out of town, taking a few days off and relaxing with some friends in Florida. She explained to Mike that she really didn't have the time to coach Randy and him, but could remember from her own business start-up that they should be thinking of making a list of all the start-up expenses that would be incurred, including assets that would have to be purchased. Also, they should reduce to dollar amounts the source of their expected revenues and prepare a monthly cash flow projection. She also said that she wasn't sure about approaching Harry either, since she really didn't know him. Her CPA was the friend and contact for Harry, so she would have to make that decision. However, she did not mind asking her CPA about it. She even added that she would try to contact her CPA that day.

Mike was excited that they might get to talk with Harry again. He immediately replied to Liz, thanking her and saying he owed her a big favor and didn't know how he would ever repay it. He was even more surprised to get an immediate reply from her saying there might be a way and that she would contact him within a week or so to discuss it.

The race was definitely on for both Mike and Randy.

CHAPTER FIVE

BIG PROGESS

Randy was anxious as he finished the day's work at the library construction site at approximately 4:00. He immediately texted his partner, Josh, and asked if he could meet him at the Home Depot five miles from the job site. Josh replied that he would drop what he was doing and be there in ten minutes. They met in Randy's truck and began some serious soul-searching.

Randy began, "Josh, I know you are one of the best landscape contractors in town, and I am honored to be partnering up with you; however, this thing of starting our own business is a serious one. I need to know if you are sure you are willing to take the risks of doing it. For example, we don't even know how much money we will need, and how sure are you of steady, profitable work? Do you have any money to put in the new business, and are you willing to risk it? I need to know these things before we go any further."

Josh smiled and replied, "Well, Randy, you will have to be the business guy in this deal if we are able to put it together. I am good at bidding the work and, I have some good sources for work that we can do. I also am good at supervising the labor folks. This is what I like to do and want to do, so all the business aspects will have to be done by you. But I can tell you that I have enough saved up to keep myself going for at least four months. Since I don't have a family yet, it doesn't take a whole lot for me. I could take my 401(K) money from my company if I had to, and that is $30,000. Of course, I would have to pay a lot of tax on that if I do withdraw it. But I am willing to do that if I have to. I also can borrow money from my Dad if I have to. He has retired, and was pretty successful. He has already said he would be willing to lend me up to $50,000 if I needed it to get the business off the ground. He said I could just pay him interest only for up to five years if I needed. So those are things I can do to help get the business off the ground. I really want to do it, and I can leave my job and get started in the next thirty days at the longest. Are you ready?"

Randy was surprised by Josh's matter-of-fact remarks. "Well, for a guy who doesn't know anything about business, you have sure covered a lot of business information in a hurry. I also have a retirement plan and some regular savings, probably a total of about $40,000, so I guess I could also make it a while with no salary also; plus, my wife has a great job working at St. John Medical Center. So, tell me, Josh, how much in revenue do you think we can get right away?" Josh did not hesitate, "At least $10,000 per month."

"We will need a trencher, backhoe, small tractor, and other miscellaneous equipment" Randy added, and asked "have you priced any of that stuff lately?' "No," Josh replied, "but my guess is we can get used equipment that we need for about $40,000. It will push $100,000 if we buy all new." Then we should look at the used equipment to get us started," Randy concluded. "I know a used equipment dealer and will see what they have that we could use. One more question, Josh, and that is how much do you think we will have to pay our labor force?" Josh thought a moment and said, "I know some real quality people we can get, but it will take a minimum of $15 per hour. Should I go ahead and talk to a couple of them?" "Yes, please," said Randy. "You got it," replied Josh.

Randy added, "My friend, Mike, and I are trying to set up another meeting with the nice guy in Fayetteville to help us get our financial plans organized. We aren't all that sure he will take time to do it, but we are trying." Josh did not seem hopeful when he replied, "My Dad was with a big corporation for years. Maybe he would have some advice for us. It won't hurt for me to ask."

Mike's day had been fitful. He had not heard from Liz, but he realized that he shouldn't expect to hear so soon. Everyone wasn't going to drop what they were doing to fit into his schedule. He had called his wife, Heather, to see if she could take time when he got home to talk about his possible business in detail. Heather agreed with enthusiasm. Mike was encouraged by her comments. He had not been certain at all that she would support the idea.

Mike was about to clear his work area and head home when an email arrived from Liz. It was awesome news. She had received a reply from her CPA that Harry Hanson was open to a possible meeting with Randy and him. Apparently, Harry was amused by the request and not at all surprised. He had said something to the effect that he knew these two guys were going to have a lot of questions and wasn't too surprised they were running into difficulties. He had also told Liz's CPA that he liked Randy and Mike and could tell they were honorable young men that were trying really hard to get their new ventures going. He told the CPA to relay the message to Randy and Mike they could call or email him at any time.

Mike's blood pressure was definitely above normal as he called Randy immediately to let him know. Randy, on his way home from meeting with Josh, answered immediately, "What's up big guy?" Mike's excitement was clearly at fever pitch as he exclaimed, "Guess what? Harry Hanson says he is willing to meet with us!" "No way!" Randy virtually shouted. "When are we meeting?" Mike responded. "Well, I don't know. I just got the word from Liz. Should I call him, or do you want to do it?"

Randy told Mike, "You should do it since you have done all the heavy lifting to arrange the chance to meet with Harry. In fact, I am hanging up so you can call him right now. I am taking a few days off from work, so set it up any time you can."

Mike immediately called Harry's number, but got only his voicemail. He just then noticed the time on his phone as 6:00. Harry had probably gone home for the day. He would try again first thing in the morning.

After dinner that evening, Mike and Heather began discussing the possible new business. Mike was still excited about the meeting with Harry as he related the day's events. "Heather," he asked, "How do you really feel about starting this business?" Heather did not hesitate with her response, "I would not be truthful if I said I am not a little scared by it, but I do have confidence in you. You are obviously good at what you do because I can see the promotions at your job. I have also heard the owners of your firm say how competent and dependable you are and how much the clients appreciate you. So, that part doesn't scare me, because I really believe you would be successful in the long run. What does scare me is the money part of it and how it would affect our kids. I don't want to jeopardize their well-being. Have you thought any about how our household budget would be affected and if we will need to really scale back? I know we have about $8,000 of savings, but that would not last us very long. Would you need that to use in the business, and do you know how soon you could start earning revenue?"

Mike tried to appear confident as he responded to her concerns. "Well, I won't need much start-up money because all I really need is a good desk-top and lap-top and maybe a good server for client backup and storage. I am thinking I could get by with $7,000 initially. I can even start by working out of our house. We have the spare bedroom I could use for an office until business is good enough to rent an office. Maybe I could borrow the money for that, but I haven't asked anyone about it. Harry likely can tell me more about this. The thing that is most frightening to me is the uncertainty of revenue. I have no clients of my own and don't have a clue how long it might take to obtain one or more, do work for them, and then be able to actually bill and collect for the work. Based on our savings of $8,000 and my Simple IRA at work of $17,000, we would have only about a four-month window. Now, that is scary."

Heather appeared thoughtful. "You know. I have been thinking while you were explaining this, and I just wonder if Mom and Dad might lend us some money if we had to have it. They are nearing retirement, but both have had good jobs for years now. I am pretty sure they have some money saved. Maybe we should ask them about it. Also, I may be able to work at least part-time at the accounting firm. They have always said I could come back to work there if I ever wanted to. My sister would love to watch the boys for a few hours each day and earn a little money at the same time. They both will be in school all day in the Fall anyway. What do you think?"

Mike was overwhelmed that Heather seemed to have such determination, apparently even more than he. He answered, "Heather, that is just awesome of you. Not only your willingness to ask your parents about a possible loan, but going back to work. You are actually giving me more confidence that we can pull this off. However, I am hesitant to ask your parents to get involved. I would be pretty miserable if something happened, and we couldn't return their money to them as promised. However, it may be good to at least ask their advice about this. As for you returning to work, are you sure you would be okay with that?"

Heather seemed calm as she replied. "I would be good with working again if I knew the boys were okay, and I do trust my sister with them. She is very caring and would love to keep them. She is staying home with her little guys that are ages two and four months, so she can't go to work for a while. I am sure she would jump at the chance, plus it would be just for the summer until the boys are in school. After that, she would only need to keep them if I had to work extra for some reason. Anyway, you need to help the kids with their baths and get them into bed. However, before you go, you didn't mention that we have a credit card with almost $25,000 of credit on it. We can use that if we get in a jam."

Mike thanked Heather for her ideas as he left the room. He could not help but recall the events of the day and how it had started out so dismal, but had ended on such a positive note.

He said to himself, I can't really comprehend what BIG PROGRESS the day has brought.

CHAPTER SIX

GAINING STEAM

Randy could hardly take time to eat dinner as he related the day's events to his wife, Vicky. "Vicky," he said. "I am getting so excited about the business. Do you have any words of advice for me?" Vicky seemed lost in her thoughts for a while, but responded after a long silence, "Randy, I know how good you have become at your work, and I am so proud of you. I am excited for you; however, you know that I am in the medical field, so I can't be of much help to you. I also love my job, so I can't see me wanting to leave it to help with the business. In fact, I hope to be asked to assume my department head in a year or two. Although, I am willing to do whatever I can with the time I might have. I am worried that you can get the money you need to get the business going. Do you have a plan put together?"

"I am just now starting on it," Randy eagerly replied. "Do you know an easy way I could start itemizing my income and expense and equipment? "You might use Excel," Vicky recommended. "It is easy to change and move around your numbers on it. I use it at work, so I can show you how to use it. We even have it on our home computer."

After a quick tutorial from Vicky, Randy began to enter what he knew on the Excel spreadsheet. He first entered the estimated revenue that Josh was confident he could generate and then showed the cost of the two laborers at a hopeful $15 per hour. He knew he would need gasoline for the equipment and two trucks, and based on his own experience, added an expense of $800 for this. Randy knew that there would more to payroll costs than just the gross wages, but he didn't know what this might be. He then realized there would be repairs and maintenance on the trucks and equipment and added an expense of $500 for that. Then it dawned on him that he didn't know if the work Josh had mentioned would require any special supplies that they would be expected to pay. He also didn't know if they would have to provide medical insurance, or even if Josh needed it. Randy was thankful that Vicky's job provided their medical. He began to realize there were so many things he was missing that he wasn't going to get very far with his schedule this evening. If only they could see Harry soon, that would be such a relief. He remembered as he shut down the computer that they had not followed up with Freddy Simon's daughter-in-law, the banker at Regency Bank. Mike and he would soon have to contact her and arrange a meeting. He hoped they would be much further along and better informed when that time came.

Mike arose early again. He felt much more positive after his visit with Heather the night before and remembered that he might hear from Harry today. He immediately began racking his brain for a possible client or project. This was now his biggest source of concern. He really had to have something to do right away because the cash reserve was not great.

Mike forced himself to concentrate on the present when the phone rang and it was a client with a software issue. He immediately accessed the client's system by remote connection and started searching for the problem. He was focusing on the project so intently that his phone rang three times before he realized it was Harry returning his call. He was able to catch Harry before he disconnected and said, "Good morning, Harry. Thank you so much for calling me back."

Harry laughed and said, "Well good morning to you, Mike. I am sorry I missed you last night, but had left to go to the Trout Unlimited meeting when you called. I understand Randy and you have discovered there is a lot more to starting a business than figuring out the legal entity you will use and its tax implications. I wanted to warn you both when we met before, but then decided it best to let you digest this at your own pace. I knew you would need a lot more help from someone, and I sure don't mind helping if I can arrange the time. I am leaving in two days for a fly fishing trip in the Smoky Mountain range of North Georgia and Western North Carolina, so my time is limited right now. Of course, I will be available after I return if you can wait a week or so."

"We are getting critical on time, Harry." Mike quickly interjected. "Any options for working us in before you leave? Randy has taken a few days off to work on his business, and I can probably get away too".

Harry checked his digital calendar and said, "I can meet later this afternoon if you guys can make it here by 3:00. You would have to leave soon to make that. Otherwise, it would have to be tomorrow right after noon. I will have only a couple hours starting at 1:30. So the time would be limited tomorrow. I have nothing after 2:00 today, so we could go on after 5:00 if we needed to. That would be good training for you after you get the businesses up and running. Entrepreneurs get accustomed to working past five quickly."

Mike glanced at the computer time. It was almost 10:00, and they would have to leave by 11:00 to make it to Harry's office by 3:00. He was sure he could finish the remote session in fifteen minutes and ask his boss for the rest of the day off for personal reasons. Mike said, "Okay, Harry, we will be there at 3:00. I will contact you if we run into traffic problems, and I can't thank you enough for letting us come on such short notice"
"Don't think a thing of it, Mike. I look forward to seeing you

guys about 3:00, but don't get in too big a rush. I will be here when you get here, even if it is later."

Mike dialed Randy and rapidly relayed what had happened. Randy informed Mike, "I am on my way to the Chamber of Commerce to pick up a publication they have for small business resources. We can meet at Highland Mall and leave a car there. See you there at 11:00."

Mike was able to finish the remote session and went to ask his boss for the rest of the day off, but his boss was out of the office for the day, so Mike told an associate to let anyone looking for him know he had taken the day off for family reasons. He thought it would be so neat if he could just leave his job and work on his own business full-time.

Mike arrived at Highland Mall at 10:45. Randy pulled alongside him five minutes later, and they were on their way. "Mike," Randy chirped, "You know what, we seem to be **gaining steam** with our crazy ideas."

CHAPTER SEVEN

MORE THAT WE DON'T KNOW

Randy and Mike sped away for their hurried drive to Fayetteville. Randy began their conversation with "Well, I am thankful we are getting to see Harry, but I had hoped to get a little bit better organized so that I don't look like a complete fool." Mike laughed and said, "I am sure there is **more that we don't know than what we do know.** But Harry is a very helpful person and I feel he will at least tell us what we don't know. Even if he can't tell us everything we need to know, he can point us in the right direction."

They arrived at Harry's office building at 2:45 and went straight to his office. He greeted them with a firm handshake and asked them to give him five minutes to finish a complex email he was sending to his daughter. "She works for a big company in Atlanta and had sent a request for guidance on a complex accounting transaction. I need to get the answer back to her while I have my thoughts organized. She is assistant controller for her company, even though she never finished her degree. I guess she heard enough from me that she is a pretty good accountant."

"Okay guys, I'm ready to talk now, so tell me what you have been up to?" Harry asked as he wheeled around in his chair to face them. He seemed at ease and in no hurry as first Randy and then Mike revealed what they had done, what they had thought, and that they now realized how little they knew about this idea of starting their own business.

"Well, it is very good you have learned there is a lot you need to learn, and apparently very quickly," Harry grinned as Mike concluded his story. "Mike," he said, "let's talk about your situation first, as I think you have fewer parts and will take less time to cover. Based on what you have told me, you are lacking in several areas. First, you should be able to itemize exactly what hardware and software you need to function, allowing for more capacity than what you think you will need. You should be able to tell me where you can get the best price for it and whether vendor financing is available. If it isn't, you will have to use the credit card you mentioned to fund it. You should also be able to show what expenses you will have each month. Those, coupled with the equipment payment and your personal living expenses will tell you exactly how much revenue you have to generate each month. You ought to set up an Excel spreadsheet and do a twelve-month projection to reflect expected revenue and expenses. That will reveal how many months of deficits you can fund before using up your savings of $8,000. You didn't say if you had a retirement plan or not, so I would like to know if you do."

Mike quickly replied, "I have about $17,000 in a Simple IRA plan, but I am not even sure I can get that out." "Thank you, Mike," Harry responded, "and yes you can access that money. However, if you have had the account less than two years, the early withdrawal penalty is 25%. If over two years, the penalty is 10%." "It would be 10% then," Mike offered.

Harry continued, "Retirement account funds are very expensive to obtain for people your age. First there is regular tax and then the 10% penalty. So, the total tax bill, including state, could be over 40%. However, you can view it as an emergency fund should you need it. It may also help you in discussing a loan with your wife's parents. Perhaps you could borrow from them, if they are agreeable, dedicating the retirement account to repay them if the business doesn't make it. Interest on the loan would be minor compared to the tax and penalty on the retirement account distribution. However, there is one other possible source of capital available to you that you haven't mentioned. How long have you owned your personal residence?"

"We have been in our house almost eight years," Mike answered.

"Then you likely have some equity over your mortgage balance," Harry quickly added. "If so, you can inquire about refinancing it, or acquiring a home equity line of credit. Even conservative lenders will consider 50% of your equity on a line of credit. This would add more cushion to your cash flow reserves and give you access to cash for unexpected business and personal expenses, that inevitably will occur. In fact, you should add 10% of your total expense budget for contingencies and miscellaneous uncategorized expenses. I can assure you they will occur."

Harry paused, seeming to take time to choose his words carefully, "Mike, I don't want you to think I am being critical of you, but I must say what is on my mind. It is meant to help you, so I hope you won't take offense to what I am about to say, and that is I wonder if you are really committed to doing this venture. You obviously haven't done anything to pursue business, to generate leads, or gauge the demand or interest in your circle of contacts. Projecting expenses is fine, but without revenue it is all for naught. This is particularly crucial for you because you have a limited time-frame in which to achieve break-even status. I will also offer you my opinion on retaining your current employment while you do this. In short, I don't think it will work. You will find yourself torn between doing your present job in order to preserve your revenue stream and taking time to work on your business start-up. My experience is that you will not wind up doing the things that must be done to start your business and ultimately will give up on the idea, leaving you frustrated and disappointed for perhaps the rest of your life. How do you feel about this issue?"

Mike sighed and replied, "You have not offended me with what you said, and you are absolutely right about it. I need to either commit to the challenge of starting my IT company or just be content to be an employee for now."

Harry seemed so genuinely interested and concerned for him that Mike was somewhat humbled. Harry then said, "You know what I think, Mike. I say you should immediately start making contacts with friends and business associates asking for their business and any referrals. You might be surprised at the response. Most folks love to help someone that is taking the risk of a new business and is sincerely asking for work.

However, you must first make the wrenching decision that you are going to go for this, no matter what. Why don't you really think about this while Randy and I brainstorm his progress?" Mike agreed, "I really do need to be asking myself some tough questions."

Glancing at his watch, Harry noted that it was 4:30 and asked, "Do you fellows need a break? I have pop and water in the refrigerator if you would like something." They all agreed a five-minute break would be good so they could stretch and collect their thoughts. Harry said, "I will take a minute and let my wife know I will be running a little late tonight. I learned years ago that it is best to let her know my plans than to just show up late and unannounced."

Harry ended his phone call, and immediately asked, "Well, Randy, where are you in this process? You seem to be somewhat more committed than Mike at this point, but did I detect a slight sense of doubt?" "I think you likely did," Randy admitted. "I have just this past couple days gained more confidence with the help of my partner and wife, but to be honest, I am still scared that I don't really know the business end of this, and will fail due to this lack of knowledge. I was hoping you could help me overcome this fear."

Harry grinned and responded with, "Randy, I admire your honesty and your fear is good in that at least you recognize your weakness. Besides, fear grips the heart of every entrepreneur, and I personally believe there will always be an element of fear long after your business is established and profitable. You see, Randy, there is a possibility of every business failing, even those that are currently profitable. The road to success is filled with failures. So, I hope you will always retain a healthy fear, and respect, for those roadblocks, hurdles, and unexpected twists and turns that a business owner faces daily."

Harry paused to allow Randy to speak, but Randy simply said, "It helps to know this is something I must learn to deal with and live with on a daily basis, and I can see that a certain level of fear of failure is probably good to keep me on my toes and be constantly alert for hazards."

"I think that is a good observation," Harry continued. "Business owners are constantly facing events and making decisions that can make or break their operations. A good healthy respect for failure is key to making sustainable business decisions."

"Let's get down to your specifics now, Randy," Harry continued. "My assessment of your situation is that you have a capable, confident partner with some financial resources. You and he also seem to understand and accept the roles for each of you in the operations of your business. You also seem to have a supportive spouse, a very important factor for all of us. Even though she has a career of her own and does not desire to work with you, she brings a good income and health insurance to the family, which is extremely important for your personal financial stability. You also have savings and a retirement account, so it seems to me you could sustain at least six months of personal living expenses without having to withdraw funds from your business if you are faced with that requirement. But again, try to avoid withdrawing from the retirement account unless you have no choice. We have already discussed the high tax cost of securing those funds. You didn't mention earlier whether you have credit cards that would allow you to secure cash with or if there is any equity in your house."

Randy seemed lost in his thoughts, but did respond, "We probably do have some equity in our house because it was in shambles when we bought it six years ago. We have completely refurbished it and added many improvements both inside and out. I am not sure about the credit cards because we have charged some of the improvements on our credit card. It probably doesn't have much credit left on it, but I will find out tomorrow just how much it does have. I really think the equity in our house would be at least $30,000 to $40,000 though."

"You are going to face a tight cash flow situation, Randy," began Harry. "At a minimum, you will need sufficient cash to cover your labor and operating expenses such as fuel, supplies, and so forth until you can collect for the first month of services. You have also indicated a minimum of $40,000 of equipment. You will also have to pay payroll taxes on your employees as you go. I can also say that you will more than likely be required to at least pay a substantial amount to secure liability insurance and workers' compensation. You will almost certainly be required to provide proof of this insurance coverage before some of your potential customers will allow you to work for them. You ought to locate a good insurance agent in your town that is familiar with your industry. They will be able to give you the options for coverage and payment. But remember, workers' compensation is required by state law." Harry seemed to have finished on the subject of insurance, but added, "One last thing before we leave the topic of insurance. Be absolutely positive that the insurance person you choose has the ability to help you with bonding. Not all are, and this could become very important for you.

Many general contractors and governments require bonding on their projects."

Randy's head was beginning to spin, but he managed to regain his composure somewhat to ask, "What do you think the insurance and payroll taxes will cost, Harry?"

"Payroll taxes consist of several different parts," Harry replied. "Regulations of the Internal Revenue Code require employers to withhold federal income tax and the social security and Medicare tax from their employees' wages at the time of payment. The states have similar requirements. These are sometimes referred to as statutory withholding amounts, because they are mandated by legal statutes. The employer is also liable for certain payroll taxes as well. For instance, the employer is required to match the social security/Medicare tax. So, 7.65% is withheld from the employee's pay and the company contributes a matching amount of 7.65%. This total, plus the federal withholding must be paid electronically either at each pay period or monthly. There are steep fines for not doing this within the number of days allowed, which is generally three days. If not paid by the company, the IRS can assess any member of management that had the ability to make sure the taxes were paid; however, this rule applies only to the amounts withheld from the employees. These are often called trust fund amounts. The state withholding is usually paid monthly and most states now require it to be paid electronically as well".

Harry caught his breath and added, "There are two additional employment-related taxes, both federal and a state unemployment tax. State unemployment is by far the higher of the two. State unemployment tax reports must be filed and paid quarterly. The federal reporting is on an annual basis, with the report, Form 940, due by January 31, for the preceding calendar year. However, a deposit must be paid at the end of any quarter in which the aggregate liability exceeds $100. Again, the federal deposit must be made electronically and the states are moving towards electronic reporting and payment as well. These taxes are the sole responsibility of the employer and are used to meet unemployment claims. Each state has its basic initial rate, which can be increased or decreased by them as each company develops a history of unemployment claims."

"Oh, by the way, I almost forgot to mention that there are ceiling amounts for the federal employment tax and both the federal and state unemployment taxes. The federal ceiling increases every year, and is well over $130,000 at this time. The state ceiling varies by state of course, but the range would fall between $15,000 and $25,000 in most states. The federal amount is $7,000, assuming state taxes are paid in full, and the rate is only .7%."

Randy's eyes were as big as saucers as he exclaimed, "There is no way I can keep up with and do all this! Can't I just let my employees be independent contractors and let them deal with their own taxes?

"Unfortunately, no, you can't Randy," Harry immediately told him, "and let me explain why. First of all, the Internal Revenue Service has addressed this issue with regulations that define the difference between an employee and a contractor. If the employee is required to report to work at times and places set by the employer and if the employer supervises and directs the work of the worker, also providing them with all tools and equipment, then the person is most definitely classified as an employee and withholding rules apply. You might think, well I can get by with this anyway. However, what if you must terminate a disgruntled person? Could they not contact the IRS and claim that you should have withheld the taxes? Remember, a contractor has to pay the full 15.3% employment tax, so some are very surprised when treated as contractors and they have their tax returns prepared. They inevitably owe more than they thought possible and become desperate, perhaps seeking someone such as yourself to blame. They might even go to IRS and claim they thought the taxes were being withheld. An event such as this would lead to substantial fines and penalties that could cause you a future shipwreck. And what if that same angry person went to the state unemployment commission to claim unemployment benefits? The state would ask who the last employer was and there you go into deep trouble. So, don't even think about trying to classify true employees as independent contractors. Of course, these rules don't apply to specialists or subcontractors that perform occasional services for you. I think you will be able to tell the difference."

"Okay, you have convinced me," Randy grinned, "but I still don't have even a clue as to how to do all this, so what am I to do, Harry?" Harry couldn't hide his amusement as he told Randy, "There is a very simple answer to this dilemma. It is called a payroll company. There are companies, both local and national in scope, which provide services for business operators like you are soon to be. They will compute your payroll and payroll taxes, prepare paychecks and direct deposit transfers, all quarterly and annual payroll tax reports, W-2 forms, and also draft your payment of payroll taxes and see they are paid on a timely basis. Their fees are very reasonable. I strongly recommend you go with one of these firms. You will need every possible minute to obtain projects and supervise their timely execution. The last thing you need is to be bogged down spending countless hours with payroll. Payroll is the easiest thing to outsource you will encounter. Two national outfits are My Pay Solutions and Paychex. I also know of a good local payroll company in your city. It is Midwest Payroll. You can find them all on the web."

Mike had sat quietly through the entire discourse, but interrupted, "Harry, will I need a payroll company like Randy?"

"Well, not immediately, Mike," Harry answered. "At least not until you hire your first employee, and then the same advice given to Randy will apply to you. Until that time, you won't need to do payroll. Since you are a single-member LLC, you are not required to receive a salary. You are, however, required to pay your expected tax liability on a quarterly basis, including your federal employment tax of 15.3%. So please budget for this. These quarterly payments can really sneak up on you if you aren't careful. The quarterly estimates payments, as they are called, are due on April 15, June 15, September 15, and January 15. You can obtain these forms at irs.gov; however, my recommendation is for you to work with a good small-business CPA to advise you on the proper amounts to pay each quarter. In fact, both Randy and you need to locate a good accountant advisor soon. You will need all the help you can get. You can ask any of your business friends for a referral and also professionals such as insurance agents, bankers, and lawyers. Your state society of CPA's will also have a directory on their webpage that lists CPA's willing to work with new clients. They are also categorized by the type services they can or will offer. Remember when choosing a CPA that you need one that works with small business start-ups. And, in your case, Randy, one who is well-versed in preparing the type of financial statements that insurance companies require for bonding. They must be prepared utilizing the percentage-completion method of accounting. You can verify that with Liz, as I am sure she has dealt with this issue in her construction business. It is also very important to choose a CPA whose personality and style are in harmony with yours. You must be able to enjoy working with this person and trusting them beyond doubt. Choosing the right accountant for you is a crucial decision. Any questions at this point?" Harry concluded and glanced at his watch.

"I do have a question, Harry," said Mike. "A friend of ours that owns a restaurant has offered to introduce us to his daughter-in-law, who is president of Regency Bank. She apparently works a lot with small business owners. Should we try to meet with her before we have done our cash flow projections, or hold off?"

"Good question, Mike," Harry replied. "I would say to hold off, for a couple reasons. First of all, you can't be really sure if you can or will be willing to carry through with this until you see how the numbers shake out. Second, you won't know what to ask the banker for until you complete the projections. So, I say you definitely wait."

Randy asked, "You didn't mention the cost of insurance, Harry. Can you give any insight to that?"

"Randy," Harry answered, "I could do some educated estimating for you, but I would prefer you get some accurate numbers from the insurance person you need to select very soon. Suffice it to say, the cost of insurance in your business will be a major one."

It was nearing 7:00 P.M. and Harry asked again if there were any last questions, as he would need to leave for home soon or call his wife and let her know he would be even later.

Mike spoke up quickly, "Harry, assuming I do muster up the courage to take your advice and really go for this, what is your advice for me on using the cash and house? I mean, in what order should I try to line up the funds to meet my expenses until I get profitable?

"I have every confidence in you, Mike," Harry confirmed, "and that is a great question." I think you would first use the savings, then the equity in your house, then credit cards, and lastly borrowing from family and friends, with your Simple IRA as a safeguard to repay the family and friends if the business doesn't make it. Actually, I think this would also apply to you as well, Randy."

"We really need to get out of here and let you go home, Harry," Randy chimed in at that time. "We are so appreciative of the advice you have given us and really don't know how to thank you, much less return the favor."

"Well guys, you both are welcome, and you can return the favor by working hard and making your businesses a good success. That would make me very proud of you. And by the way, I would like for you to email a copy of your cash flow projections when you have them completed. I want to look them over for any obvious problems before you start showing them to other people. In the meanwhile, you can also call or send an email if some big issue comes up you need to ask about. I will be back from my fly fishing trip next week."

After shaking hands and thanking Harry again, Randy and Mike began the long drive home. It had been a long day, and would be even longer after their four-hour drive. They were quiet for a while until Mike broke the silence, "We have had an exhausting day, but at least **we know a lot more about what we don't know now."**

Then Mike's phone rang - it was Liz.

CHAPTER EIGHT

COMMITTED!

"Hello, Liz," Mike answered as he lifted the phone to his ear. "I am surprised to hear from you. I thought you were having fun there in sunny Florida."

"I am," Liz laughed. "I have to go home tomorrow and get back to the real world. The reason I am calling is that a friend of mine in your area needs some help. She started an upscale restaurant downtown about a year ago that has been successful. Her name is Ruthann, Ruthie for short, and she is in dire need of a more sophisticated software and network system. She can't track orders and manage costs of her food and beverage items. Her volume has increased to the point that she is losing control. Do you think you can help her?"

Mike was stunned. "I actually have helped a couple restaurants with their systems," Mike managed to finally reply. "I would sure like to talk to her and see if I can help her."

"Great," Liz said. "Are you going to do it for your new business or your current employer? I guess it really doesn't matter though. She needs the help either way. I will give her a heads-up and you can let her know who will be billing her. But she is in a panic. Can you get with her tomorrow, or no later than Monday?"

Mike found himself grasping for things to say, but managed to respond, "I will contact her in the morning and see when I can go see her and the restaurant. I will likely be acting under the banner of my own company, Horizons IT Consultants, LLC, but will know for certain by the time I meet with Ruthie. I have actually heard good reports about the restaurant although I have never been. This will be exciting."

"That sounds awesome, Mike!" Liz replied, indicating she was pleased. "Make me look good for referring you, and one last thing before I get off, I want to talk to you in a week or so about upgrading my server and adding remote capabilities for more on-site job accounting from my superintendents. But I can't talk now; the rest of my crowd is waiting on me for our last dinner on the beach. Talk to you soon, and good luck with Ruthie."

"Thanks, Liz, and enjoy your last evening there," Mike quickly added as they both hung up. Mike was speechless, and curiosity was killing Randy.

"What was that all about?" Randy asked. Well, you just won't believe it!" Mike responded, his excitement growing by the minute. Mike recounted his conversation with Liz as best he could. He was clearly astounded by the sudden turn of events, and it was obvious.

"I am excited for you, Mike," Randy declared, "but you still have a hard decision to make whether you are ready to commit to this. Remember what Harry told you. But while you are on a roll, don't forget that my company will probably need your help also. My partner and I don't have a clue about all that. I expect you to give me a deal, of course," Randy laughed.

"Don't worry, I will give you a very special hourly rate," Mike promised, "and as for the big issue, Liz and you have pushed me right over the edge. I am **committed,** 100% sold out, with no looking back. In fact, I am going to **call** Heather right now and just make sure she is still good with this insanity. She has been so supportive that I really believe she will be."

Mike reached Heather and went through the entire day's events with her. After a considerable time, he put down his phone and reported to Randy, "Well, Heather is on board 100%!"

Randy was excited by Mike's obvious change of heart and show of new determination. "I congratulate you, Mike, on your new confidence and enthusiasm. I know you are going to do great. I plan to sit down with Vicky as soon as possible and go over the numbers with her. But first I have to put them together. I am glad I have a few days away from work. I see now that I will need every possible minute of every day to work on the new business. Josh also wants me to call on some of his proposed customers, on top of everything else. I guess I should not complain about that, since it is nice to have potential customers to call on. I remember what Harry said about that, which is that without revenue none of the other matters. So, he is basically saying sales and marketing are very crucial parts of a business start-up."

Mike interrupted, "I have a question for you, Randy, and it is whether or not you are ready to leave your job and devote all your time to getting open."

Randy seemed determined when he replied, "Yes, I am. I have decided to tell my Company what I am doing and give them as much time as possible to replace me. I would like for them to let me go as soon as possible. Even though I still have lots of hurdles to overcome, I can't wait any longer to make it my sole priority. I can only hope and believe that I will be able to put it all together, but I must try."

"You are tough, and inspiring, Randy," Mike praised, "and I am glad to have you for support."

Randy and Mike talked about all the challenges that lay ahead and the work that was staring them in the face, arriving at their homes about midnight. They both now realized that they were **committed**. Scared, but **committed.**

CHAPTER NINE

A MAD SCRAMBLE

As tired as he was, Mike could barely sleep during the night. His thoughts were brimming with excitement, with questions, and thoughts of what the future held. The alarm jolted him to reality. He knew he had to get to the office and he knew he must find time to meet with Ruthie. He also had to make serious inroads on the financial projections. He also realized he must start marketing his services, but didn't want to do this until he had told his boss. Anyway, you looked at it; life was going to be **a mad scramble** for the foreseeable future.

Heather soon arose. "I will call the CPA firm and see if I can speak to someone about part-time work," she offered. "I also thought I would visit Mom and Dad and feel them out for a loan, if you want me to. Also, have you thought about setting up a page on Facebook to let friends and family know about your new business? I will also get the word out to all my friends. Who knows, some of them may able to point you to someone who needs your services. I can also start your monthly cash flow statements. Of course, it will have lots of blanks, but we can add those as we figure out what they are. What do you think?"

"I think that is all great, Heather, and I can't even start to tell you how much I appreciate your help, but I just don't think it is right to start promoting my own business while I am still employed at the company. Do you agree?"

"Mike, that is very honorable of you and, of course, you are absolutely right; however, if our family is going to be dependent on this new business, then I just naturally want to start doing everything I possibly can to help you make it successful."

"And you are more than justified in feeling that way, Heather. I think I need to tell my boss right away, if you agree."

"I agree. Please let me know as soon as you do."

Mike could feel the adrenalin forming as he drove to his office. The thoughts of talking to his boss and to Ruthie were racing through his mind, and his stomach was beginning to feel nervous. Maybe, he thought, this is what Harry was talking about. If it was good to feel a little scared, then he should be in great shape, as he was downright frightened by it all. He could see that his boss, Tim, the sole owner of the company, was already at the office when he arrived. Tim was a great person and very fair and honest, but Mike did not know how his resignation would be received. He could only hope for the best.

Mike, felt he should talk to Tim immediately and went straight to his office. "Good Morning, Tim. May I talk to you when you have a few moments?"

"You bet, Mike. How have you been? I have been so busy the past week or so, I haven't even been able check in with you."

"Tim, I have something very important to discuss with you. I have made a decision to at least attempt to start my own IT business," Mike stammered as he noticed his heart pounding. I have enjoyed being here with you, and you have been very fair to me; but, I just believe I will be happier with my own firm."

Tim did not reply for what seemed like an eternity to Mike, but then asked, "Mike, are you sure there isn't something I could do to change your mind? You are a very important part of our company, and it is an understatement that I sure would hate to see you go. You are due a raise soon, and I certainly would not object to implementing it now. I am open to your input on the salary range that would be satisfactory to you also."

Mike could not really believe what he was hearing, but managed to assimilate his thoughts to reply, "Tim, that is very kind of you, but I think I have reached the point at which I can't turn back. In fact, I am having trouble focusing on my work here, which is why I needed to talk with you today. I will stay as long as you need to find someone to replace me, but to be honest with you; I want you to know that I will also be working on my new venture in the meanwhile."

Tim seemed to be in deep thought as he sat in silence with Mike. "I really don't think I can find someone quickly with your knowledge and experience. If you are absolutely positive I can't do anything to change your mind, then I have a proposal for you. You don't know that I just signed a contract yesterday with Payne County to totally upgrade their IT system at the courthouse. We have to start the project next week to be done by their deadline date. It will be tough to do, especially without you. My proposal is that I continue to pay your regular salary for thirty days, knowing you will be spending some time each day on your start-up. After thirty days, I will offer to utilize your time for twenty hours a week for another sixty days on a contract basis at the same hourly rate as your salary. This will help me get the Payne County work done while I am finding someone to replace you. The benefit for you is flexibility and time to devote towards your business. It also gives you some steady income for a few months until you can develop your clients. The only thing I ask is that you not solicit any of my existing clients for their business. If any of them approach you wanting to change, you agree to discuss it with me, and give me the opportunity to convince them to stay. Actually, there are a couple that are not so profitable for us, so you are free to talk to them if you like. Perhaps you can make money with them, since your overhead is likely to be fairly small at first. What do you think, Mike?"

Mike literally could not believe his ears. His fear of a confrontation with Tim was starting to subside, and Tim's proposal seemed to be a great solution for him. He just could not fathom that the discussion had gone the direction it had. "That seems to be a gracious offer, Tim. When can we start on that basis?"

"Right now, Mike, but if you think about all this overnight and would like to discuss staying on with us for a while, I am open to do that any time. If you don't let me know otherwise, I will assume we are working on the proposal. I will even send you an email to document it. I will also call the two accounts that can transfer to you and recommend they do that. Just give me a couple days to do that before you contact them."

Mike agreed with Tim and thanked him for the proposal. They shook hands and Mike went to his office. He was nervous now with excitement and immediately called Heather, letting her know what had happened and asking her to move ahead at full speed with her ideas.

Randy had not slept well during the night either. He arose at 6:00 to be ready to talk with Vicky and get her final approval. Assuming she was still agreeable, he was determined to throw caution to the wind, even though he didn't relish the thought of telling the two owners of his present company. While they were both nice and had treated him well the past seven years, they also could be rather hard-nosed when they were in adverse circumstances. Vicky soon arose, and when she was dressed for work, Randy asked, "Vicky are you still sure you are comfortable with me and the business? I did have a good meeting with Harry last night and am even more determined to go for it, unless, of course, you object."

"Well, I would not be honest if I said I have not had some second thoughts about it all; however, I can see it is very important for you to do this. I also have the utmost confidence in you to succeed with it. I guess I am just having the normal fear of the unknown. Anyway, I did compile our monthly budget last night for you. I know you will need that as you complete your cash flow projections as you call them. So, I say go for it!"

"Thank you, Vicky!" Randy muttered as Vicky left for work. The monkey was now squarely on his back. He decided to wait until he returned to work on Monday to talk with his owners. Remembering that Josh wanted him to talk to some potential customers, he texted Josh, who replied quickly saying they could drop by the two customers in the afternoon and he would let him know when. He then decided to work on the cash flow projections. At least he had some idea about payroll and payroll taxes, thanks to Harry. He had also learned that Josh needed insurance and that the two proposed employees were not accustomed to having insurance provided. He wondered if the new Affordable Care Act would change that. Randy added the supplies expense Josh had told him were necessary to get the work done for the customers that hopefully were still onboard. It hit him that he hadn't discussed their own work trucks with Josh. Fortunately, he owned his old truck and his company had been giving him an extra allowance to cover his use of it in the business. He wasn't sure about Josh, so he sent a text to Josh who replied his truck was owned by his company, so they would have to figure out that situation. Randy thought they could buy a decent truck for something in the neighborhood of $15,000, but that was his first big surprise, an added $15,000 to the capital needed. Surely, they could finance the truck, he thought. Randy added $1,000 per month to cover operating costs of the two trucks, but he had no clue on the insurance costs for a business vehicle, thinking the liability part might be expensive. He sure needed to talk to an insurance person, but didn't know who to contact. Harry had said it was important to work with someone who also did bonding, he remembered. Perhaps Mike knew someone, so he texted Mike, who replied that he didn't know anyone, but maybe Vicky could ask her contact at the CPA firm. He would get back to Randy as soon as he could. That reminded Randy that he didn't have the cost of a CPA in the projection. Harry was adamant Mike and he arrange for the services of a CPA, and for himself, one that knew the ropes of preparing statements for a bonding insurance company. He also now realized that he would need someone to do customer billing, accounts payable, payroll, etc. as he forced himself to not become discouraged by what he still didn't know and understand. Mike should be able to help with some of that, since Vicky worked for a while at the CPA firm. He decided to call Mike and see what he thought about all that. Mike did not reply, but Randy left a detailed message.

Randy called his equipment dealer contact to firm up the exact cost of the equipment they would need to get by on a bare-bones basis for a while.

"Hi Travis, this is Randy checking back on the equipment I called you about a week or so ago."

"Yes, Randy, and thanks for calling back. I have three of the pieces you need in stock, but not the other two. However, I have a dealer in Georgia that has them. I can have them within forty-eight hours if you need them that quick."

"No, Travis, I am not quite that far along, but I do need a pretty firm number on the cost," Randy responded.

"It won't be more than $45,000 at the outside," was Travis's answer.

"Can you finance it for us?" Randy inquired.

"No, I don't do financing or leasing, but I have two sources that might buy the equipment and lease it to you, if you can convince them of your ability to pay. However, since you have no track record, you might have your work cut out for you. They usually give you a percentage off the rental fee to apply towards the purchase when you are ready to do that, even if it is at the end of the lease," Travis volunteered.

"Please ask them if you don't mind," Randy requested. "I am working on our capital and am just not sure if we will have the money to pay cash."

"I sure will do, Randy, and will let you know as soon as I can," Travis promised as they disconnected.

"Hello, Mike, and thanks for getting back to me," Randy anxiously answered his phone call.

"Hi, Randy," Mike began. "Heather has a couple leads for us on insurance agents. She says one of the partners at the CPA firm, Morton & Co. recommends them as being professional general agents, which apparently means they work with different insurance companies, and also means they can find the very best deal for us. Even better for you, they both work with contractors and know how to help get the bonding Harry and you talk about. Heather set up a meeting for me next Tuesday, and you are welcome to go with me. If not, I will email the contact info to you so you can schedule something that works for you."

"Just awesome, Mike, and I will try to make it with you, but please send the info. Who knows what will be happening by next Tuesday. Any input from Heather on the accountant? Will her firm work for us?"

"Heather thinks that Morton & Co. is a very established firm with a great reputation. The trouble with them is they are so busy that it might be a problem getting in with them on short notice. Heather says they have one partner who is big into working with contractors. He even is a member of Associated Builders & Contractors, which is apparently a trade association of independent contractors. It would be great for you if he would take on your business. Should I ask Heather to do some snooping for you? For some reason, she doesn't think my business will be that complicated, leaving a lot of room for selecting a CPA. She thinks someone who just emphasizes small business work and doesn't mind a start-up would be just fine for me. She says there is one partner at Morton who would fit my bill, and she is going to see if he is interested. By the way, she would also like to pitch you on doing your bookkeeping, payroll, etc., so get ready for a sales pitch."

"Awesome, man," was all Randy could come up with. "What would I do without you?" "The feeling is mutual, my friend," Mike offered back quickly.

Randy noticed a text from Josh, asking if they could meet at Freddy's Barbecue for a quick bite and then call on the two potential customers. Randy replied that he would meet him at 11:45 sharp.

"Well, look who drifted in," Freddy laughed as he greeted Randy and Josh. "I thought you guys had struck it rich in your new business and were eating lunch at the country club these days. And where is your other buddy, Mike, I believe is his name?"

"Freddy, you are either dreaming or making fun of us," Randy shot back. "We are still trying to figure out how to get started. Mike is working on his project, but isn't joining us for lunch today. Josh and I are meeting so we can strategize on meetings with some potential customers after lunch."

"My daughter-in-law never heard from you, but says she is more than happy to talk to you about things. She is busy, so you better call in to get a time set up."

"We have been afraid to call her because we don't have everything put together yet, but we will definitely need her help, if she is willing," Randy explained. Josh and he ordered and got down to the issues at hand.

"The folks we are meeting with are friends of mine," Josh began. "I have done their work for years now, for my company of course. They will be willing to go with us, but they are also shrewd business operators, so they will probably try to get a reduced rate from us. However, the volume will be nice and steady. They are property managers for both commercial and residential properties and are probably the largest one in town. So, all we really need to do today is to let them meet you and see that you are a real, live person. We also need to be prepared to give them a start date, our billing terms, and convince them we have the horsepower to get the work done. My guys are still teed up to come over with me. Of course, this all will not make my company owners happy at all, but these guys are customers that I brought in, so I don't feel bad about it at all. In addition to that, the workers spend 80% of their time on these accounts, so the company won't need them anyway."

"I think we can give them a 15% discount and still bill them at least $9,000 a month," Josh concluded.

"Wait a minute, Josh," Randy interrupted. "There is no way they will use $9,000 of our work during the winter months. In fact, I doubt if they will use us at all during that time."

Josh seemed a little uneasy as he answered, "True, the services won't be that much in December through February; however, I can do special landscaping projects, irrigation repair and maintenance, and some odd jobs during that time. I bet we can get at least $3,000 per month during that time."

"This tells me we have to land some new construction work to get us through the winter months," Randy reflected. "Do you have any contacts with builders and developers," he asked.

"No, I don't," Josh admitted. "But we can ask these guys for referrals when we meet with them. Also, don't forget that my workers aren't used to working full-time in the winter, so our expenses will be lower."

"Okay," Randy spoke, as he reflected on all this. He suddenly realized how crucial the monthly cash flow statements were that Harry had so adamantly insisted be prepared.

"What about your truck?" Randy continued.

"It is not too old, but has lots of miles, Josh answered. I would be willing to pay them about $10,000 for it. If not, my friend at the Ford place says he has a truck that is three years old, but in good condition he can let me have for $12,000. It will work just fine for me. He says he can also get me 2.9% financing, so that might be the way to go."

"How would you pay the $10,000 for the other truck?" Randy quizzed.

"I have enough cash to pay it, or my Dad might lend me the money," Josh quickly replied. "However, I hate to get him involved unless we really need him. As I told you, he is willing to lend us $50,000 with interest only, if we need it, so I don't want to interfere with that unless it is absolutely mandatory."

"Right," Randy heartily agreed. "I say you get the truck from your friend and get it financed. The business can make the payments on it. That is something we should ask the insurance person about too. I want to hold your Dad's generous offer as our source to meet a really unusual and unexpected financial problem. We need to get going if we are to be on time for our meeting."

"We will be calling your daughter-in-law soon," Randy told Freddy as he paid the bill. "I only hope she is patient with us start-ups."

"Don't worry," she knows what your types are all about," Freddy laughed.

Both meetings went well for Josh and Randy. They agreed to start work May 1, which was only three weeks out, and that thought scared him more than a little. It turned out Josh was right on with his estimate of the fees, which in fact had to be discounted 15%. Still, it would give them the base to get started. The customers also gave them contact info for two builders and a large development firm. Randy was excited, but scared, just as Harry had warned him. He knew the **mad scramble** was on for the foreseeable future, and that all the fun was just getting ready to start.

CHAPTER TEN

NO LOOKING BACK

Mike was still reeling from his meeting with Tim, but realized his relief, having his intentions out on the table. He also felt there was **no looking back** at this point. However, at least he could now focus on all the tasks and challenges. He managed to contact Ruthie by email and arrange a meeting for 4:00, before her evening rush began. He could feel the excitement growing as he realized he was getting ready to make his very first client proposal. He hoped he could gain Ruthie's trust. He also sent a quick email to Liz, letting her know about his meeting with Ruthie and that he was forging ahead with his own business. He also dropped a hint that he was anxious to discuss the special project she mentioned. He was able to browse the Dell website, identifying the equipment he would need. He decided he would go with just a good laptop and desktop, avoiding the cost of his own server, figuring he and his client could use the Cloud for all that. These items, along with a printer, scanner, and fax combo should hold him for a while. He owned his own cell phone, so no extra cost for that. Software that he would need would include a remote access module and whatever accounting software Heather or the CPA suggested. The maximum cost appeared to be no more than $10,000. He realized that he would not be able to purchase equipment on account and then sell it to clients, but hoped he could get by with asking clients to just pay for their own equipment and software. He would establish credit with Dell and others as soon as possible and, hopefully; also qualify for their dealer discounts. This would potentially allow him to realize some additional profit from the equipment and software purchased for clients, or simply use the discount as a selling tool in order to help secure the work that could be billed hourly.

Mike was now able to take care of his job duties with ease, since he could now focus on the tasks at hand. He could hardly believe what was happening as he left for the restaurant to meet with Ruthie

He was soon at the restaurant, which was definitely an upscale dining establishment, located in an area of downtown that was being re-developed by leaps and bounds, known by the locals as the Blue Dome District. "Hi Ruthie, I am Mike", he began. "Thank you for meeting with me, and I sure appreciate the opportunity to discuss helping with your project. I have just started my new IT consulting business, but I hope to convince you I have the experience to handle your needs."

Ruthie replied, "Well, I am sure you have the ability to help me, and being referred by Liz goes a long way. Nothing like a recommendation from someone you know and respect."

Ruthie got right into her problem. "I just don't have a good accounting system, nor a good system to manage my servers and the ordering process. Liz says you have worked with restaurants in the past, so I am curious to hear your recommendation."

Mike drew on his previous experience, "I have helped with two restaurant installations. One seems to be very similar to your circumstances. You need a cash register with remote stations for servers that feed orders to the chefs. The credit cards and cash are posted directly to your accounting books. You can even add inventory control if you will set up your items and enter the unit cost and quantities when you receive merchandise. Does that sound like it hits on your problem?"

"Yes, it does, Mike," Ruthie responded. "But can you give me a feel for the time it will take, and the cost?"

"I can start the installation as soon as we can get the equipment delivered. I know of two providers that we can look at also. Do you have the funds available to move quickly?" Mike inquired.

"I was hoping the suppliers might be able to finance at least a portion of it. I can put $5,000 down, and my bank might help out as well. My banker seems willing to work with me, especially since the restaurant has taken off. If all else fails, I do have a friend that has said she will lend me up to $20,000 if I get in a jam. What about ongoing expenses?" Ruthie seemed anxious as she glanced at her watch. The rush would soon begin.

"I am hoping you will engage me to do your monthly maintenance and trouble-shooting also," Mike laughed nervously. "If so, I estimate it would run an average of $375 monthly, based on my billing rate of $125. However, the initial fee will likely come in at about $5,000. What do you think?"

"Based on what some of my associates and friendly competitors have said, your fees seem reasonable," Ruthie acknowledged. "I should be able to pay that out of cash flow, if you will give me little while. Can I pay your fee in two monthly installments?"

"Yes, that will work for me." Mike agreed. "Should I go ahead and price the hardware and software for you?"

Ruthie did not hesitate, "Yes, please do, and give me a call tomorrow. Also, can you ask about financing?"

"I will check it all out and get back to you as soon as possible," Mike promised. "I will also get going, so you can get back to work. Looks like you might have a good night. Thanks so much for your business!"

Randy, went home after meeting with the new customers and began working on his cash flow statement. Vicky had obviously thought of everything in the personal budget, and he could see that they were spending $5,000 per month, including about $400 on a credit card, reinforcing his fear that the amount available to borrow on it would not be that great. He added $1,500 to cover a lease or loan payment for the equipment and another $400 for Josh's truck payment. He was anxious to see what the cost of insurance and accounting would be, but could see cash flow would be very tight, based on everything he knew at the moment. Randy realized soon that he had entered everything into the cash flow worksheet that he could at the time and resigned himself to listing possible contacts for projects. The fear of failure crept into his mind, which at this point, he was learning to deal with.

The weekend would slow things down for him, and he thought perhaps he could talk to Heather about the accounting costs. He also was getting anxious about revealing his plans to his Company owners, acknowledging his fear of the unknown. He decided to call Mike and see if he had told his boss about his plans.

"Hello," Mike seemed upbeat as he promptly answered Randy's call. "What's up?" he asked.

"I was calling to see if you talked to your boss and if you got the restaurant job," Randy quickly began.

Mike rattled off the events of his day and was obviously in an optimistic mood.

"That is just awesome," Randy replied. "That encourages me a lot. Maybe my outcome with the owners will go well. I also need to know what I need to arrange for Heather to take care of my bookkeeping and payroll."

"I will talk to her and get back to you today or tomorrow," Mike assured Randy.

The weekend vanished for Mike as he worked on the restaurant project for Ruthie. He located the hardware and software and sent the pricing to her, which was $14,000 for the equipment, including software and $4,500 for his fee. He tried not to be anxious, but asked her when they could get started.

Heather had talked to the CPA firm and she could start in a week with them. Based on her hours, she hoped to net about $2,800 per month, after taxes and paying her sister to watch the kids.

"Heather," Mike asked. "Randy has asked if he could talk to you about taking care of his bookkeeping and payroll." Heather answered, "I will have to talk to my supervisor first to be sure we can do that for him. It will be Monday before I can do that."

Heather continued, "I was also able to talk to Mom and Dad about your new business. They are of course excited for us and are open to helping us financially. They have accumulated some saving and investments, but think they still have to be cautious with their money. However, they are open to talking about helping us if we need the help. I told them it would only be if we really needed short-term help."

"Thanks, Heather. You are so much help and give me a lot of confidence," Mike said appreciatively.

Mike and Heather spent much of their weekend setting up a Facebook page for the new business and sending texts and emails to friends and family. Mike also started developing his own webpage. Time was now of the essence. He knew deeply in his heart there was **no looking back** at this point, and his optimistic nature was at least temporarily returning.

CHAPTER ELEVEN

HURDLES, HURDLES, AND MORE HURDLES

Randy's weekend had been tense, as he alternated between worries of securing the mandatory new customers to reach break-even, as Harry had so strongly explained to him, and talking to his bosses on Monday. He had made a list of potential customers to call on, but that was about all he had accomplished.

He got up even before the alarm sounded at 6:00; determined to get an early start. He hadn't been to work for a few days now and the apprehension was building to what he felt an unbearable level. He dressed quickly and left the house before 7:00, stopping at his favorite early-morning coffee spot, Java Don's. There were none of his friends in this morning, so he made an effort to strike up a conversation with Norman, who managed the shop. "Norm, I am worried to death right now because I am trying to start my own lawn care and landscaping business," Randy muttered half-heartedly.

"Seriously?" Norm replied. "That is really neat, but why are you so worried?"

"Well, to be honest, I am scared that I can't get enough business to pay all the expenses and that I might not make it," Randy replied meekly.

Norm seemed thoughtful as he replied, "Well, I have never even thought about starting a business, but I sort of understand your fear. But maybe I can help by telling all my customers that you are starting your own business and need work to do. You never know, some of them just might need your help."

Randy was amazed by Norm's comments. Why would Norm offer to do this, or even care about Randy's business? As he recalled Harry's comment about people wanting to help, he managed to respond, "Norm, you don't know how much that means to me. Thank you so much for offering to help. That is really nice of you. Maybe I can return the favor sometimes."

Norm smiled and said, "When you talk about coffee with all your future customers and employees, you can tell them Java Don's is the best in town."

Randy was sincere when he told Norm, "You can count on that, Norm."

Randy began thinking of what he would say to his bosses at work when he told them of his plans. He certainly was not looking forward to having that conversation, but knew it had to happen today. He would probably tell Ted, the 50% owner that handled personnel and business issues. He was the one that seemed to be in the office most of the time.

Ted's car was in the parking lot when Randy arrived at his office. He got another cup of coffee and went straight to Ted's office. "Good morning, Ted. Do you have a few minutes to talk?"

"Good morning to you Randy. Are you rested up and ready to go, after all that time off? We got approved for the irrigation and landscape project at Wilcox Industries. That will keep you busy for a while."

"Ted, there is something I need to tell you. I have decided to start my own small business," Randy muttered anxiously. "I hope you are not disappointed because I have enjoyed working with you guys and appreciate all you have done for me. I won't leave you in a jam either."

Ted seemed to be shocked by what he was hearing. "Randy, are you sure you want to do that? Do you know how risky it is and how difficult it is to make a profit? You will end up in bankruptcy!"

Randy answered softly, "Yes, I know how risky it is and how tough it will be, but it seems like I have to try it."

Ted, who seemed to now be irritated, shouted, "Well, then you can count on us making it difficult for you. We will compete with you so you won't get any work and even if you do, you won't make any money on it. You also had better not contact any of our customers. In fact, you can just leave right now. Don't talk to any of the employees, now or in the future."

Randy could not believe what he was hearing. His thoughts were confused and he even felt faint. "Ted," he finally managed to ask, "Are you sure you don't want me to stay on until you find a replacement for me? I promise I would do a good job and work hard as long as I am working for you."

"Randy, please leave our building. You are no longer welcome here, and we don't need your help," Ted was almost screaming by now.

What about my final pay for this pay period and my unused vacation," Randy managed to muster up the courage to ask.

"We will mail your final pay check to you on payday, but it won't contain any vacation pay. You will lose that as far as I am concerned. Now please get out of my office!"

Randy was in a stupor as he found his way to his truck, without realizing where he was or what he was doing. His emotions were running out of control as he started home. His thoughts were racing from one thing to another. He had not expected his boss to be happy about his leaving, but Ted's reaction had been over the top. Every doubt that he had ever had about starting the business was now resurfacing. He felt uncomfortable physically, and scared. These feelings and thoughts were intensified by the fact that his bridge with the former company was now burned, completely. The reality of it all settled in on him as he drove back home.

"Vicky'" Randy anxiously said when Vicky answered her cell phone. "I have some bad news about my job." He then told his wife of the intense meeting with Ted.

"I am disappointed for you, because I know you didn't want it to go that way; however, there is nothing you can do now. You can't control how others act, so you just need to double up on your efforts and plans. I am proud of you for not being mean to Ted, even though he deserved it. I have so much confidence in you, and I hope this makes you just that much more determined," Vicky replied in a comforting, but yet stern, manner.

Randy was somewhat encouraged by Vicky, but still visibly upset. He decided to check in with Josh and see how he was doing with his job.

"Hi Randy, what's going on today?" Josh answered in a jovial tone. "Josh, you won't believe what happened with Ted today," as he reiterated, step-by-step the painful experience.

Josh seemed totally unconcerned as he interrupted Randy, "I am sorry you had a bad time with Ted, dude, but that doesn't surprise me all that much. He is known as a hard-nose all over town. Anyway, I went ahead and broke the news to my guys and they weren't all that happy either. However, it isn't hurting them that much, and we agreed to stay together until the first of the month when our contract starts. At least they didn't have a fit. Anyway, I got to run now. Got a problem on a job site. Keep me posted."

Randy's cell phone rang a minute later and it was Mike. "Hi Mike," Randy answered. Mike could tell that Randy seemed down. "What is up?" Mike replied. "You seem a little down today."

"That would be the understatement of the year," Randy responded in the most discouraged voice Mike had ever heard him speak. "I had a nightmare experience with Ted this morning," Randy continued and told Mike the ugly details of his encounter."

"Whoa!" Mike exclaimed, "What a downer that must be. What are you going to do now?"

"Well, since I don't have any really good choices, I am going to take Vicky's advice and double down on my business. Starting right this minute, I am going to focus intently on all issues needed to make my business a success - 24/7. I need to talk to Heather about my accounting today if I can. I also have to contact the equipment dealer about getting our equipment on order and figuring out how to pay for it. I am anxious to meet with the insurance agent tomorrow and see what I need and what it costs. I also think we should schedule a meeting with Freddy's daughter-in-law. Freddy talked like it might take a while to get in to see her. In the meantime, I am going to start calling on potential customers and letting everyone I know be aware of what I am doing. I may even take on some regular lawn maintenance to generate some immediate cash flow. That isn't what I want to do for the long-term myself, but who knows, I might even get enough of that work to hire a manager to run it for us. I am even willing to do the work myself to get us up and running."

Mike sat in silence while Randy bared his soul. He then simply said, "Randy, you will make it. I admire your resolution, and I know you will be a huge success. I do have some info for you on the accounting issue. Heather says her firm can do your accounting, including customer billing and vendor payments. However, there seems to be a kicker. She says that if the firm does your books, the partner who deals with contractors, bonding, etc. can't do your work. It has something to do with the firm not being able to issue statements when they prepare the books. They refer to it as not having independence, and it applies to all accounting firms. So, you will have to decide which way to go. You could try to find someone else to do your bookkeeping and use the partner at Morton & Co., or you could let them do that and try to find another CPA to do the financial reporting. Confusing enough for you?"

"Well, it is not a total shock to me that there are complications," Randy seemed sarcastic as he laughed. Just another crisis for me to resolve. What does Heather think about it?"

"She refuses to comment, since she is involved. It will have to be your call, Randy," Mike said apologetically.

"Sounds fair enough, and I understand. I will think about it, but it would help if I knew the costs, so I could plug them into my cash flow projection," Randy responded hopefully.

"That is a reasonable request, and I will ask Heather to work on that today and tomorrow," Mike promised.

"Thank you, Mike," Randy concluded as he reminded Mike of the meeting with the insurance agent the following day.

"That is the other thing I need to talk about," Mike said. "I have a conflict with a client at my company, so I had to call and reschedule the meeting for me, but told the agent, Steve Palmer, that you would come anyway. I will text you his contact info. Is that okay with you?"

"Sure," Randy replied appreciatively. "I am anxious to find out about all that, as I know it will be a big item for me."

"You will like him," Mike assured Randy. "He seems to be interested in us and very easy to talk to. He also comes highly-recommended by Morton & Co."

Randy immediately got in his truck and drove to a potential customer's office. He spent the rest of the day calling, texting, and personally visiting as many friends and business acquaintances as he possibly could. He was amazed at the encouragement offered by most of them. Even the customers, who made no offer of work, did offer him wishes of good luck and promised they would help if they could. By the end of the day, he had somewhat recovered from the trauma of his encounter with Ted and other challenges of the day. He felt a strong resolve, but knew he would have more **hurdles** to overcome.

Mike was excited when he saw Liz was calling. "Hi Liz," Mike answered. "I have been hoping to hear from you. I am working hard to take care of your friend, Ruthie. Her project is coming right along."

Liz then told Mike the good, and bad, news. "Mike, I am committed to implementing the new IT system, but after talking to my controller, we have decided to wait a few months. We just started two elementary schools and a retirement center, so we are just swamped right now. I hope you will be available when we are ready to proceed."

Mike was obviously disappointed, but managed a positive reply. "I am sure happy for your new projects. It's obvious you and your staff will be too busy to work on the IT project for a while, so I will just sit tight until you are ready. I will be anxious to start, of course, as soon as you are."

After talking to Liz, Mike was shaken with what he considered bad news. He had been counting on the nice fee form Liz's business to fund his start-up time. That would obviously have to wait a while. He decided to call Ruthie and see if she was still on target for her new system.

"Hi Ruthie," Mike asked enthusiastically as she answered his phone call. "How are you doing? I thought I would just check in and see if you had time to see about financing for the new project."

"Well, not that good," Ruthie replied. "My banker said he couldn't lend me the money until I completed at least six months of profitability, showing enough cash flow to repay the loan. I can see my cash flow is growing by leaps and bounds, and I am sure I can make the payments, but he doesn't see it that way. I guess I could ask my friend for a loan, and she would probably do it; however, I kind of hate to borrow from her, and I know she would want a hefty interest rate. Do you think the equipment seller would finance it for me, Mike?"

Mike had trouble hiding his disappointment, as he answered, "I did check with Dell and they would consider giving credit, but of course, you would have to pass their credit check. I can send over their credit application if you like."

"Okay, I guess it is worth a try, but I am not too excited about getting approved, considering I have only been in business for less than a year," Ruthie said in a subdued tone."

Mike downloaded the credit application and emailed it to Ruthie, as he thought of Randy and the day he had, not to mention his own bad news. He could see that Randy and he were facing **hurdles, hurdles, and more hurdles.**

CHAPTER TWELVE

ONE DAY AT A TIME

"Good morning, this is Steve Palmer", said the insurance specialist as he answered the phone call from Randy.

"Hi, Steve," Randy replied. "I just wanted to confirm our meeting at 10:00 that Mike set up. He said that he had cancelled, but you could meet with me."

"Of course, Randy, and I am looking forward to visiting with you. You can even come on over any time that is convenient for you. I am here at the office all morning."

"In that case, I will head over right now. See you soon, and thanks," Randy replied quickly. Randy was filled with resolve and determination, realizing he would just have to do everything possible, and take things **one day at time.**

Randy was soon sitting in Steve's office, a professional, but yet unpretentious office in the city's most prominent office area.

"Thanks for seeing me, Steve," Randy opened to start their meeting.

"You are sure welcome, and I am more than happy to see if I can help you. I am interested in hearing where you are on your new business, if you don't mind giving me some background."

Steve sat and listened very intently as Randy told him his story up to that point. Randy was impressed with Steve's attention and focus on what Randy was saying.

"Do you have any specific questions about me or our agency at this point?" Steve finally spoke.

"The folks over at Morton & Co. told me about you. Mike's wife is going back to work there," Randy answered. "I think I just need you to educate me on what I am looking at for insurance coverage and costs and also give me any pointers for business you can. Also, I am in dire need of business if you possibly have any leads for me." Randy was now becoming much bolder in his search for business."

"Sure," Steve responded. "First of all, I can find coverage for all your needs, and I do work with contractors to secure bonding. I write coverage for several different insurance companies, so I can find the right fit for you. You will, of course, need workers' compensation for your employees, as that coverage is required by state law. In fact, the State provides a fund to provide coverage for businesses that can't obtain affordable coverage in the market place. Your partner and you can opt out of the workers' compensation coverage if you like. Many small business owners do opt out, especially if they have medical and disability coverage otherwise. The rates for workers' compensation are dictated by the type of work that your employees do. I can tell you from my experience, you are in one of the higher categories.

You will need general liability insurance for protection against any civil liabilities. In addition, you will also need some coverage for replacement of equipment in the event of theft or destruction by accident. This should include owned and non-owned coverage for any vehicles used in the business, including those of your employees.

Your workers' comp premiums can be paid monthly in advance if we use the state fund, so that might be your best option at this point. I am guessing your premium won't be over $250 monthly if you and your partner don't need coverage. We can likely finance your other insurance over a nine-month period; however, you will need to pay 25% down. I won't know the exact premium until we submit it to the carriers; but, since you mentioned you need to complete your cash flow projection before seeing the banker, I think it would be safe to use a total premium of $5,500, based on the level of business and type of equipment you mentioned earlier. The liability insurance will be a reportable type policy, based on revenues. The base premium is set based on expected premiums, but can be increased at the end of the policy period, which is one year, if your actual revenues have been larger. You will need to keep this in mind if your business grows during the first year, which I know you hope will be the case.

As for business pointers, the biggest problem I see with the construction contractors is lack of good cash management and poor bidding practices. When business is good, there is a tendency to overspend on equipment or personal items, resulting in inadequate cash when business takes a downturn. So, my advice is to be very frugal for the first few years, even if you do seem to have plenty of cash. This also will assist you greatly in securing bonding, if you do wind up needing that. My guess is that you eventually will. The problem with bidding is either the lack of considering all costs when bids are prepared, such as insurance for instance; or, just being too optimistic. We all tend to think we can do our work more quickly than is realistic and at less cost than is actually the case. One bad job can actually put you out of business, and I had a very large and successful client go bankrupt a few years back. They under bid a project, and it was one that was a little more complex than what they had been doing. They were unable to finish the job and had to cease business. The owner, who had other business interests and extensive real estate, had guaranteed the bond and bank debt. He had to file bankruptcy and lost everything. So be very careful with your bids, and especially if the job has any new or different twists that you are not familiar with."

Steve paused for a moment and then continued, "One final thing, Randy, if you do plan to do bonded work, your accounting is very important. You will need to have a good job cost system because you will have to report income and expense by job to the bonding company. Your choice of the right accountant is very important. I know you have been talking to Morton & Co., and they are a very good firm. However, if Mike's wife works there and does your books, they probably can't do the review financial statements that are mandatory for bonding. Apparently, their ethics rules don't allow them to both do the books and then report on the financial statements. I can also give you a couple other people in town that are good with contractor accounting and whose work is accepted by the bonding carriers. Just let me know if you need their names.

Well, I know I have talked a lot. Do you have any questions at this point?" Steve concluded.

Randy seemed to be a little overwhelmed by all that Steve had shared with him, but finally managed a response, "First of all, thank you so much for all the information and advice. You have sure given me a lot to think about, even though some of it frightens me to no end. I know it is good to know of the pitfalls. At least I have a chance to avoid them if I know about them. I will take the contact info for the two CPA's if you don't mind. I think I would lean towards Heather keeping my books and letting another firm do the statements."

"There is one more thing," Randy added. "Any suggestions for how I could generate some leads for work? I understand if you can't do that."

Steve grinned and said, "I don't blame you for asking that, and I can give you maybe some general ideas. I will give you a list of about five general contractors in town that you can call on. I also would call on the real estate developers, and there are maybe six or so in town. Both these should be good contacts for you, although it might take a while. As soon as you think you can afford it, you might look into joining Associated General Contractors or Associated Builders and Contractors. You would meet a lot of good contacts at both of them. I belong to Associated Builders, or ABC, and one of my associates is a member with Associated General Contractors. The main thing is probably to let all the folks you have worked with in the past know what you are doing, but I will pass your name along to anyone I can. I don't have another client in your particular line of work, so I can give any referrals I get to you."

"What if my former bosses get angry with me for soliciting business and try to do something that would be harmful to me?" Randy asked.

"Do you have a covenant-not-to-compete with them?" Steve queried, and Randy answered, "No, I don't."

"Then I probably would not let that stop me. Our agency no longer does business with Ted and his company, and all I hear about them is mostly negative. They are probably going to try to make life difficult for you no matter how much, or little, you do. Do you want me to begin the application process for your insurance?" Steve finished.

"I suppose you should," Randy concluded. "We will actually begin operations in about two weeks, so I guess I don't have a choice. Please delay payment as long as you can, as I don't have much capital at this point. We won't get our first payment on the big job for two more months."

"I wish you the best in your venture, Randy," Steve offered, and the meeting came to an end.

Randy was torn between returning home to work on the cash flow statement and making calls to contacts and potential customers. He quickly decided to do the sales calls and plan to complete the cash flow work that night. He contacted three people he knew with the city construction department and one person at the county level. He also drove by two job sites and talked to the job superintendent at both sites. He felt good about the reception he was having in general; yet, there was no promise of any work at this point. Several people told him frankly they were glad he was no longer with Ted's company. He realized that he really had not known that his former company had a reputation for being difficult to deal with. In fact, two people told him they had continued to do business with his old company primarily because he was doing the work and the one who they dealt with. That was encouraging to Randy.

Near the end of the day, Randy remembered that he had not heard from Travis on the equipment. It was getting close to when they would need the equipment in order to do the work they had committed to take on. "Hi, Travis, this is Randy," he spoke as Travis answered. "Did you check on financing for the equipment for us?"

"Yes, Randy, I did," Travis answered. "However, the only thing I can do for you is a three-year lease, and that is contingent on you being able to put 25% down. And the equipment in Georgia will not be available much longer. The dealer there said he will hold it only two more days. The financing is contingent on a personal guaranty from you and your wife, as well as your partner." What do you think? We don't have much time."

"Wait a minute!" Randy exclaimed. "My wife is not involved in the business at all. She works at the hospital as a registered nurse. Why does she need to be involved?"

"Lenders want both spouses to be responsible for the loan" Travis tried to explain. "Otherwise, it would be too easy for one spouse to avoid payment, with the other spouse owning all the assets. You are fighting a losing battle on that one. This lender won't do the deal if your spouse doesn't guarantee the debt."

Randy was furious, realizing he would now have to ask Vicky to be involved with the risk of his business. He realized that he had been, and still was, so naive to all the aspects of business ownership, and was basically angry with himself for not already knowing this.

"Let me do some checking, and I will get back to you first thing in the morning," Randy said excitedly. "Thanks for your help, Travis".

Randy immediately called Josh to tell him the news. "Josh, this is Randy. How are you doing? I have some problems to discuss with you. Can you meet me at Java Don's after work?"

"Sure," Josh replied. "Actually, I can be there in fifteen minutes. See you when you can get there."

"Hi Norm," Randy gave his greeting as he arrived at Java Don's.

"Have you started the business yet?" Norm inquired. "I have told a bunch of people about you, and some of them seemed interested. I hope you can handle all the work you will be getting when they all call you."

"Well thanks, Norm," Randy replied. "I have been busy trying to get everything together, but I am running into some problems. We plan to be ready to go in under two weeks. I am meeting my partner, Josh, here in a few minutes to talk about some big stuff."

Josh arrived shortly, and asked Randy, "What has happened? You seem really up tight, Randy. Norm, has Randy been drinking too much coffee today? He seems a little messed up." Norm laughed and said, "No, but maybe he needs to drink more. It might calm him down actually."

"Josh, we have some serious problems on our hands," Randy spoke urgently. "First of all, we are about to lose the equipment in Georgia if we can't commit to buy it in two days. And not only that, Travis says the person that is willing to lease it to us wants 25% down and wants Vicky, you, and me to guarantee it personally. What do you think about all that? For one thing, we don't have the down-payment of roughly $12,000. I plan to see the banker about a loan on my house, but that isn't going to happen by day after tomorrow."

Josh seemed very concerned, but also calm, as he spoke. "Why don't I use some of my savings to cover this for now, Randy?" We can worry about settling up for your half later. As for the guarantees, I don't know much about all that, but I guess I really don't mind doing it. I can sort of understand the person doing the lease us wants to have risk on it, so we can't easily ignore paying the money back. Besides, if our business doesn't make it, I will be completely broke anyway. And finally, I really believe we are going to make it, so it won't matter that we personally guaranteed the lease. I bet this won't be the last time we hear about personal guaranties in our business. I say go for it.

Plus, I have some good news for you. I have gone to see the two developers my customers referred us to. One has a new development going in here in town and the other one has a big project in Prattville. They both said we could bid on the dirt work, sod, and trees. Both would be done early next year, which is perfect for keeping us busy during our slow season."

"Josh, you just amaze me," was all Randy could say. "I wish I could be as calm and confident as you. I hope Vicky will go along with us." Randy then told Josh all his news for the day.

"Hi Sweetie," Vicky seemed cheerful as she arrived home. She immediately sensed something was bothering Randy. "You seem to be worried," she continued.

"You diagnosed me correctly as usual," Randy confessed and related the situation with the lease guaranty. "I couldn't blame you if you don't want to do it, but apparently, we can't get the equipment now if not. What are your thoughts?"

"I know nothing about business, so I suppose I believe this is a normal request for small business owners. I sure don't like risky situations, and this whole thing about business ownership scares me, no doubt. However, I am willing to do it if required for you to get started. Also, you mentioned not long ago that you might need to borrow on our credit cards. We do have one with about $10,000 of cash advance credit on it, if you need it to help get the equipment."

Randy didn't know if he should be happy or remorseful. "Thank you, Vicky. I will be sure this doesn't cause you any trouble."

"Oh by the way, I told my boss today about you, and he said you should call on the maintenance supervisor at the hospital. Apparently, they use outside vendors for some projects at the hospital grounds."

Randy began plugging in missing amounts in his cash flow projection. He could see he was at a deficit of $2,000 per month, and that was before any salary for Josh and him. He then added an estimated $75 per month to pay Midwest Payroll, or whichever payroll company Morton & Co. recommended. He also texted Josh and asked him if he could meet him somewhere at 10:00 with a check for the $12,000 down-payment. He also told Josh he would reimburse him for $6,000 as soon as he could get an advance on his credit card. Josh replied that he would do it and Randy realized he did not even have checks for the account they had opened.

Worry was working its way back into Randy's mind, but he recalled that he had promised to take the adversities **one day at a time**, and right now was a good time to remember that.

CHAPTER THIRTEEN

IF IT WERE EASY....

Mike had completed his cash flow projection except for the insurance cost, which Heather thought might not be all that much after asking one of the CPA firm partners. He stewed about the delay with Liz's project and the uncertainty with Ruthie's work. He also didn't know how long Tim would be willing to allow him to work at his company. He was on the verge of feeling sorry for himself when he remembered a saying he had heard from a veteran business owner. This person had said, in talking about business trials and tribulations, **that if it were easy, everyone would be doing it**. The comment, while seeming humorous at the time, was now deadly serious. Mike now realized why starting and owning a business is not for everyone, and maybe not for many. Mike admittedly was now humbled by the process. Yet, his resolve was growing each day.

He was encouraged by the fact that the two clients Tim had offered to transition over to him had graciously accepted and that should add about $500 a month to his revenue. He also had received a tremendous amount of support from friends and business associates. He had even had promises for small amounts of work from two friends, who said their companies needed IT help. Heather's firm also said they could mention his name to some clients, even though they were committed to their existing service.

Mike believed that with the work he had, assuming Ruthie got financing, that he could survive for at least eight or nine months now with the savings Heather and he had, and the cash he could obtain on his credit card. He considered himself so lucky to have Heather to keep his books. She would teach him to do his own billing in QuickBooks and also to enter his disbursements. She would then review all he was doing to make sure it was all correct; thus, he would have no accounting costs.

Mike could clearly see his biggest challenge now was generating the revenue, and while this concerned him, he was gaining confidence daily, based on what he was hearing from others. He had his webpage up and running as well as his Facebook page. In addition, leads were coming in every few days from various sources, some of which he had never dreamed would refer business to him.

The equity in their house was also a source of cash if needed. He thought that he would discuss that with the banker, and that he should do that soon. He had sort of been waiting or Randy and knew that Randy was really struggling with a host of problems. He then thought of Harry's suggestion to send their cash flow statements to him for a quick look before they met with the banker. He decided to go ahead and do that now, as he felt he was substantially done.

"Hi Mike, this is Harry. Hope you are doing well. I just received your cash flow and have a couple comments if you have time."

Mike replied, "Harry, I didn't expect you to call. Of course, I have time. Thanks so much for getting back to me so soon."

"I am accepting, of course, your personal expenses as being accurate, but you should not put those in the cash flow statement you present to the bank. Just show your business income and expense. The net income will then be the cash available to pay your personal living expenses. Also, since you will have some business profit, you ought to include the income tax and self-employment tax that I told you about when we met. Plus, I don't see any entry for credit card interest or credit card fees for accepting credit cards from your clients. Other than that, your statement looks pretty good. Congratulations on your good work. I see you have obtained some business."

Mike told his story of the past few weeks to Harry. "I feel silly for not thinking of the credit card interest and fees. Of course, I need to accept credit card payments if clients request that. Can the bank help me with the credit cards? I know my barber uses Apple, or Square, as they call it."

"Yes, I would investigate both," Harry replied. "I haven't heard from Randy. Is he still moving ahead with his plans?"

"He is Harry, but he seems to be running into some problems," Mike responded.

"That is not surprising," Harry said. "He has many more issues with revenue and capital than you. Guess I will let you go for now, but contact me any time if I can help with something, and all the best to you."

Mike then sent an email to Steve Palmer to see when he come meet regarding his insurance. Steve replied that he could meet at 4:00 the following day.

Mike was torn between calling Ruthie yet again to see about the financing and patiently waiting to hear from her. It had been several days since he last spoke to her, so he decided to go ahead and try her one more time

"Hi Mike," Ruthie answered promptly. "I know you are anxious to get started on the work, and I am even more anxious than you. I do have good news. My friend is willing to lend the money to me. Even though she wants 12% interest and wants it to be repaid over eighteen months, I think it will be worth it. I also think I can make the payments, so let's get started. I can get the money tomorrow, so can you pick up a cashiers' check tomorrow evening?"

Mike tried to hide his excitement, but it was obvious to Ruthie. "Of course, Ruthie, I will be over around 7:00, and thanks so much." Mike was elated. His confidence level had just ratcheted up. He decided to check in with Randy, and share his good news. He hadn't heard much from Randy the past few days.

"Hi guy, long time no see. What is keeping you so busy?", Mike began in a light-hearted manner.

"I am glad you are having a great day, Mike, but things have been tough on my end of things," Randy answered in a clearly down-trodden manner. He then brought Mike up to speed on his frantic schedule of events the past two days.

"Wow, I feel for you," Mike offered empathically. "I wish I could help, but I am barely handling my own problems. I did get the go-ahead on the restaurant project today and am meeting with Steve Palmer tomorrow. I also sent my cash flow to Harry today, and he called me not long ago. I am ready to see the banker."

"To be honest, Mike, you should go ahead and schedule your meeting with her," Randy offered sincerely. "I am not ready yet, and to be completely honest, I don't know when I will be."

"Okay," Mike agreed. "By the way, I have a saying for you, if starting a business were easy, everyone would be doing it. I found it encouraged me a little."

Randy tried to sound upbeat as he muttered, "**Yes, if it were only easy**."

CHAPTER FOURTEEN

IF IT WERE EASY... - PART II

Randy couldn't get Mike's comment out of his mind. On the one hand, it irritated him. Of course, starting a business was not easy, and he seemed to be encountering every pitfall possible on a daily basis. On the other hand, he did find some strange solace in knowing that because it wasn't easy, and in fact very difficult, then not many others could start a business and eliminate or reduce his chances of success. So, it is a paradox. **If it were easy....** Oh well....

"Hi, Randy," Heather answered. "Hi Heather," Randy responded. "I wanted to let you know that I want you to do my accounting. Since that means Morton & Co. can't do my bonding company statements, I will have to find another CPA for that. Steve Palmer gave me two names, and I wanted your advice on who I should contact."

"One of those was also recommended by my partner, so I would contact him if I were you," Heather volunteered.

"Sounds great, and I will do that soon," Randy agreed. "In the meantime, what do I need to do now in order to get set up with you on the accounting?"

Heather explained, "You will need to call or email billing info and descriptions when you are ready to get out a customer billing. I will then prepare the invoice and mail it directly form here. For now, I suggest you do this as soon as you can, so you can get cash coming in quickly. Later on, we may bill once a week, or every two weeks. That will be your call. You also need to send me personal data for each employee. I will email a form, known as a W-4 for each person to complete. I want Josh and you to complete one also, even though you will not be taking a paycheck initially. At least I will have it when you do start paying yourselves, and I know you hope that will be soon."

Heather continued, "I will also order checks from Intuit since we will be using QuickBooks for your accounting, including check writing."

"Will you have them in time for our first payroll?" Randy inquired. "We will have to pay those guys weekly, and that means the first payroll will be only two weeks from now."

Heather assured Randy payroll would not be a problem. "The payroll company prints the paychecks on checks they produce, so we don't have to worry about those. They can mail those to you if you structure your cutoff for the payroll sufficiently long enough prior to the actual payment date. For example, if you end the pay period every Friday, but hand out checks on Tuesday, the mail should work for you. The option is to pay them to have the checks delivered by courier. They also can do direct deposit if you want."

"We won't be able to use direct deposit," Randy noted. "Our guys don't even have bank accounts. So, which payroll company are we using?"

"I like Midwest Payroll myself," was Heather's response. "However, we have clients with Paychex and MyPay Solutions. I like Midwest because they are local and we have more flexibility with them. They are all about the same price, so no big advantage there. If anything, MyPay Solutions might be just a bit cheaper than the other two, but they would have a longer mail time or would charge for overnight delivery versus courier for Midwest. I think your payroll, since it is weekly, will run about $150 monthly."

"Okay, let's go with Midwest," Randy concurred. "I also think we can get by with Friday for the end of pay period and Tuesday for the check release. I know my old company handled it that way. How do you get the information from them to do my accounting?"

"Oh, that is easy," Heather informed Randy. "I simply go online to their webpage and print your reports and enter them in QuickBooks. That reminds me that you also need to set up online banking for your account, which will allow me to access your bank statements and enter that in QuickBooks without having to bother you with all that."

"Both Harry Hanson and Steve Palmer have told me in no uncertain terms I need to be able to produce statements that show each job's income and expense by job. Will what you do provide that?" Randy asked hopefully.

"Well, yes and no," Randy. "I have discussed this whole thing in great detail with my supervisor. What I understand is that you only need to do that with jobs that are under contract and that take several months to complete. The remainder of your work that is either recurring or of a short-term duration will simply be classified as service income. We can break this down any way you want, such as residential and commercial, or by type such as mowing, tree planting, etc. You can think about that and we will figure it out as we go.

For the actual contract work, we will need to assign a job number to each contract. You will need to be sure you note on your invoices or checks the job number they relate to. Of course, this is in addition to coding them to the expense category to which they belong. For example, we might code an invoice to supplies for job number XYZ. Or it might be supplies for service work, with no job number. To complicate it even more, you will have to tell me if the payroll is service or contracts. That may be easy, but you will need to think about how we can do that. I do know Midwest Payroll can produce reports broken down by jobs and service, but it will be up to us to give them the hours allocated in that manner. Finally, there are some expenses that will be next to impossible to allocate individually to each job. Some that come to mind are insurance, vehicle costs, and even supplies that are used for all jobs as well as service work. I am told that we don't have to worry about these because we can let the accountant who does your year-end statement for the bonding company do an allocation to jobs for the year. I think my partner said this is usually done by comparing direct labor on each job to total job labor for the year. But the good news is that this is one thing we don't have to worry about."

"That is good, but it sounds like we do have plenty to worry about, and it seems awfully complicated to me," Randy stated. "I hope I can do all this and still do the day-to-day work."

Heather sounded confident and supportive, "Randy, I will help you, and we will get this down to where it doesn't take much of your time, I promise. We have QuickBooks for Contractors here and that will help minimize my time and fees also."

Randy thanked Heather and left home immediately to meet Josh and get the check. He thanked Josh for his willingness to use savings for the deposit on the lease.

"No problem," Josh replied modestly. "I still have enough to last a couple more months, and I can always use my 401(K) if I have to; but I believe we are going to get a lot of work soon."

Randy arrived at the bank and asked a pleasant teller what he needed to do, after explaining his situation. "Do you need a cashiers' check?" the teller asked. Randy, not wanting to appear stupid, for the second day in a row, said, "I am waiting to hear back from the equipment dealer on that. If one is needed, will there be any problem in doing that today?"

"Yes, probably so. Our bank has a five-day hold policy on deposits. So, it will be five days before we can give you credit for your deposit and issue a cashiers' check on your account."

Randy was on the verge of an emotional fallout. Another surprise he thought to himself. Would they never end? "I will go and check my messages and come back when I know more," he answered. If not, what can I do? I have no checks on my account just yet."

I can prepare some temporary checks for you," the teller offered. "There is no charge for that."

"Thank you very much," Randy answered. "I will find out as soon as possible." He called Travis from his truck. "Travis, this is Randy. I am at the bank and it has come up whether the down-payment has to be a cashiers' check. The bank is telling me it will be five days before I can get credit for my deposit and then get a cashiers' check."

There was silence for a while, but Travis finally said, "You know Randy, in order to make this deal work I will have to send payment for the equipment in Georgia by wire tomorrow. So, if you can't pay with bankable funds, I will be at risk for that until you do. I would not normally be willing to do this, but since you are struggling so hard to get your business off the ground and might even be a good customer in the future, I will go ahead and get the equipment. I will get the lessor to email the lease agreement to you. I would say get a cashiers' check as soon as you can. You and your wife will need to sign the guaranty section of the lease and you sign as the company officer, whatever that is. Let me know as soon as you have that done, and I will coordinate the closing so you can pick up the equipment here. By the way, this is what is called a capital, or financing, lease because you own the equipment at the end of the lease. You can ask your accountant how that is handled, but essentially you treat it the same as a purchase. You show it as an asset on your books, but you also have to show the lease obligation as a liability. The down-payment will be increased for sales tax and each payment will include sales tax on the principal portion as well as interest. Again, your accountant will figure all that out, but your cashiers' check will be increased to include the sales tax. It will all be spelled out in the lease document. Any questions?"

Randy was thinking to himself that he should have expected a surprise. He had no clue he had to pay sales tax on the lease, but then again, he would own it after all the payments were made. In an attempt to sound savvy, Randy asked, "Is there another type of lease other than this financing lease that I could do?"

Travis informed Randy, "Yes, there is an operating lease that allows a pure lease for a set period. At the end of the period, the lessee has the option to buy the equipment at its fair market value; but, this lessor is not willing to do that kind of lease with the type of used equipment you are getting. He also knows you are a start-up."

"Got it," Randy finished. "I will expect the lease soon, and will bring it and the cashiers' check as soon as possible. I also appreciate your willingness to help us out by taking a chance on buying the equipment in Georgia."

Randy went back into the bank and informed the teller that he did actually need a cashiers' check and to please give him a call as soon possible to pick up the check.

"Do you need regular checks printed for your account, and deposit slips?" the teller asked.

"My bookkeeper said she would buy the checks. She said she needed checks to match the software she will be using, but she didn't say anything about deposit slips, so I don't know."

"Many of our customers who obtain checks from some other source have us do the deposit slips," the banker volunteered. "But you can let us know about that anytime."

Randy then realized he had not even thought about a mailing address for the business. He really didn't want to use his residence address but they would not have an office, at least not for now. He would have to ask Heather if he could use their office address, or maybe it would be better to get a post office box.

Randy decided to swing by Freddy's Barbecue and get the contact info for Freddy's daughter-in-law, the president of Regency Bank. "Hi, Freddy," Randy greeted him in a low voice. I came to get the contact info for your daughter-in-law. I need to see her soon."

"Well it is about time!" Freddy responded, as he slapped Randy vigorously on the back. "How is it going?" he asked as he handed a business card to Randy. "She is expecting your call, if she hasn't forgot about you by now. Her full name is Sharleen Ellis, but she likes to be called Shari."

Randy thanked Freddy and quickly went on his way. He had to let Josh know the equipment would be available soon and that they needed to figure out where they would keep it.

"Josh, do you have a minute," Randy asked quickly after Josh answered his cell. "For you, any time is good," Josh laughed.

Randy laughed too, and asked Josh, "Have you thought any about where we will keep the equipment? We will need to pick it up at Travis's yard in less than a week.

"Sort of," Josh replied. "I know of a storage place that has a pretty good rate for a space that will hold all our stuff when we aren't using it.

Randy said, "I sure don't have a better idea right now. Can you take care of getting a space for us? Save your receipt so the

Company can reimburse you for it. I think I will get a PO Box to use as our business address. I will get a key for you when I do."

Randy called Heather and asked about the mailing address. She thought the PO Box was a good idea, but also let Randy know that if he wanted a vendor to send invoices to her, he was perfectly welcome to have them do that. Her firm would not object at all.

"Just FYI for Mike, the banker's name at Regency Bank is Sharlene Ellis," Randy concluded. "I am going to call for an appointment today. I guess Mike wants to talk to her also?"

"Yes, I think he does," Heather agreed. "We are thinking we need to get a line of credit for the equity in our house, to have available if we start to run out of money before the business takes off. I will pass her name along to Mike, and good luck to you."

Randy then called Sharlene and got her voicemail. He left a message, letting her know how he knew of her and asking for an appointment.

Randy spent the remainder of the day continuing to call anyone he could think of and inquiring for work. He also called all the general contractors and the developers that Steve Palmer had given him. He was able to reach some of them and left messages for others. All those he spoke to you were nice, but so far, no work had been discussed. Josh called to let him know he had made a deal to buy a used truck at the dealership as they had discussed. His friend would hold it until they began work for the two existing customers. The payments would be about $300 per month for forty-eight months.

The next stop for Randy was home, where he immediately began putting the finishing touches on his cash flow projection. He now could fill in the blanks for insurance, accounting, the equipment lease, and the truck payment. It seemed he had just about covered everything, and he couldn't wait to see the outcome. However, the outcome was not what he had hoped. It looked like they could cover expenses as long as they were collecting for the two big jobs, with a little left over for Josh and him. This would not be enough to cover the salaries Josh and he were accustomed to, but would help a lot as they built up their business. It also didn't pay back the equipment down-payment. The scariest part was January, February, and March, when there would be very little revenue from that work. Yet, Josh claimed he had other work that could be done during that time. Randy was now getting paranoid that he hadn't landed any work. He decided to register on Angie's List, feeling that he was willing to take on residential work if necessary to generate income. He ended the day by sending his projection to Harry and asking for any input Harry might provide.

He was awake until the wee hours that night, thinking **if it were only easy....**

CHAPTER FIFTEEN

TIME IS THE ENEMY

Mike yawned as he arose at 6:15. The days were getting longer for him as he worked virtually full time for Tim and had the restaurant job now going in full swing. Fortunately, he could work at the restaurant in the evenings. He thought to himself, **time is the enemy** now. Each month that goes by with expenses in excess of the income, the closer I get to being a business failure statistic. He knew his days as a business owner were numbered if he did not get his revenue up by at least $3,000 per month. That was the infamous break-even point of which Harry had warned Randy and him so sternly. There were some nice things happening, but not enough at this point. Heather's sister had referred him to her church, which was needing a complete update on their IT system. The two clients that Tim had given him were going smoothly, and he knew they would start paying in a few weeks. Heather's CPA firm had also started mentioning him to some of their clients, and he had quite a few comments from friends and even Facebook posts that were encouraging. Mike fought back thoughts of fear and failure, but he knew the present reality was that he would eventually go broke if some of these leads did not turn into work and cash flow soon.

Mike checked his calendar soon after arriving at the office. He saw that he was meeting with Steve Palmer today at 4:00 and was glad to be taking care of that. He thought that he must call Sharlene Ellis and get on her schedule. He decided to call her right now and was surprised when she answered, "Shari speaking."

"Hi Shari, this is Mike. I got your name from your Dad, Freddy. He is a friend of mine from me seeing him so often at his restaurant." "Oh yes," Shari responded. "He has mentioned you to me a couple times. What can I help you with? "

"Well, I was just hoping you could give me some guidance on borrowing money for my new IT business. I need some equipment, but primarily I am going to need money to cover my short-fall for a while until I can get more business."

"I understand, Mike, and I just had a meeting for 2:00 today cancel. Any way you could come to my office then?"

Mike was elated and answered, "Yes, of course, I will be there" Anything particular I will need to bring?"

"You might bring a copy of your last tax return and any cash flow projections, if you have them."

"I can bring both of those," Mike concluded as they said good-bye. He was actually shocked that he had got to speak to her so easily and meet the same day. Maybe this was to be his lucky day.

Mike showed up early for the meeting with Shari. She greeted him into her nice office and spent some time getting to know him a little better and learning about his business, and its challenges.

"Of course, we would like to have your checking account business," Shari explained as she got down to business. "We offer online banking and bill payment. You can also make deposits remotely. We can also help you with credit card usage, if you would like to offer that to clients. As to your start-up expenses, this is a more difficult problem. Our regulators make it tough for us to lend to start-up businesses unless there is an overwhelming amount of collateral or personal guaranties available. However, I don't want to discourage you. Our bank is very keen on working with the small business community, and we are heavily involved with SBA lending. Why don't you let me take a look at your tax returns and cash flow projection? I actually could use your personal financial statement. By the way, you are one of a very few folks wanting to start a new business that have met with me and actually had a cash flow projection already prepared. I am honestly quite impressed with that."

"Well, I have to confess I had a lot of help with that," Mike chuckled and related the story of his meetings with Randy and Harry Hanson. "I am glad I was able to learn how to do that early on, because it has clearly pointed out to me that I will be in a deficit once the arrangement with my former boss comes to end, which could be at any time. It has been a real motivator for me to search for business, not to speak of the fact it scares me senseless every time I look at it."

Shari seemed amused, but yet very serious with her response, "Well, it may be scary, but at least you know the problem. Many entrepreneurs don't even know they have a problem until it is too late to solve it. You, on the other hand, know exactly what you are faced with. I think that gives you a much better shot at solving the problem."

"Well, thank you so much for your input and advice," Mike added. "I know you have been working with small business owners for a long time. Do you have any advice you can give me about finances and even how to seek out new clients?"

Shari appeared reflective as she gathered her thoughts. "You have already done the most common advice I give to our bank customers, and that is to analyze your cash needs and learn to live within your budget. The typical start-up is working on a shoe-string. This lack of working capital makes it a dangerous proposition. Statistics bare out the fact that 70% to 80% of start-ups in America fail within five years. The reason is lack of capital. So, in other words, it is the lack of sufficient funds to grow, meet unexpected expenses, and survive erratic revenue streams that are fatal to small business. So, I think the best thoughts I could share with you would be to watch your expenses carefully all the time and keep a cash reserve once you have had time to accumulate one. One other thing might be, to the extent it is possible in your business, to seek out recurring services in order to have steady cash flow every month. I imagine a lot of your business might be from specific upgrades and installations, but if you could come up with a service that you can provide every month, month after month, it seems to me that would help you guard against cash flow surprises."

"As for getting new clients, that is a tough one too. I know a lot of our business here at the bank comes from customer referrals. I think that is why I am always telling our people to do a really great job for whomever you are working with today – and right this minute. Happy clients or customers are our best opportunity for growth. Besides, someone who is referred is always less difficult to actually bring on board. They have a need or desire, or they wouldn't have come in or called to begin with. And, this a very important, they somewhat trust us already due to the kind words of their friend or business associate who mentioned us to begin with."

Shari seemed finished with her line of thought, but then added, "I realize you need to bring in new business right now, and I think there are a few specific things you can do. For example, we have a loan officer who is active in a trade group called Associated Builders and Contractors, which is a group of various construction contractors and related service organizations. It took him a while to become well known, but over time he has attracted quite a few nice customers and regularly secures new customers from this source. Another person has become active in the Small Business Council of the Chamber of Commerce and is also bringing in some nice business through that activity. Of course, you would have to measure the time and cost of these types of things, as well as whether or not they are likely sources of business for you."

"I wonder too if you get on preferred contractor status for electronics suppliers. I don't know of any specific ideas on this one, but what if, say Best Buy, outsources its installations, etc. With the technology as it is today, even individuals are spending large sums of money for systems at their home, and of course, they all require installation and maintenance. Or, you could choose an industry or segment that you have a lot of experience with and do direct marketing to those businesses."

"Anyway, Mike, I need to wrap up so I can get to loan committee meeting on time. Let me think of how we might support you. Here is a personal financial statement form. Completing that will help me in evaluating your situation and what we might be able to do. I don't want to encourage you too much, but we would like to have your business, and frankly, you seem better prepared than most would-be entrepreneurs. I sure wish you all the best."

"Thank you very much, Shari," Mike concluded as he rose to leave her office. "I really appreciate your time and advice. You have given me a lot to think about."

"Good afternoon, Mike," Steve Palmer greeted Mike as he arrived at Steve's office. "It is good to meet you in person. Please sit down and tell me about your new business venture."

"Good to meet you and thanks for meeting with me," Mike replied. He then proceeded to bring Steve up-to-date on all that was going on with him.

"Well, the good news I have for you is that your insurance needs are fairly straightforward and inexpensive. I think I can get the basic fire and casualty and general liability insurance you need for only about $650 annually. I can bind the coverage and you will receive an invoice for it. You can even charge it on a credit card if you like. I don't know if you have thought of professional liability coverage or not, but that is an entirely different story. It will be very expensive, if we can even get it. My other IT clients don't have it either."

"That is good news on the regular coverage, and I haven't planned to get the other. So far, no one has asked for it."

"Are you good with health coverage?" Steve continued. "And do you want to obtain workers' comp insurance or opt out of it as you are allowed to do as a business owner."

"Yes, my wife, Heather, can get medical insurance through her work at Morton & Co. when mine terminates at the company where I am working now. I also guess I want to opt out of workers' comp, since I have good medical insurance. Does that make sense?"

"You seem to be logical with your thoughts on medical and workers' comp," Steve answered.

"Do you think you need disability coverage?" Steve probed. "I have never thought of it," Mike confessed. "Well, don't feel too bad. Most folks don't. It would cover you for a certain amount of payments in the event you become ill or get injured. If not now, maybe we can talk about that once you get on a profitable basis."

"I am sure I will need to wait, as I am in the red already," Mike informed Steve. "This brings me to a question I have for you. My friend, Randy, said you gave him some business pointers and some advice and help on developing new business. I was hoping you would do that for me."

Steve laughed as he replied to Mike, "I am not sure what I had to speak with Randy about was all that valuable, but let me think if there are any pointers I can remember. I do know that the friends or customers I have that are in the service business such as you seem to struggle with growth. They tend to get really busy and think of finding someone to help them, but that doesn't seem to be easy for them at first. It is a struggle to find the right person that they can actually afford, and even if they can, the first thing you know they lose a big client and can't afford the person any longer. So, I guess I am just giving you a heads up to be expecting this problem, and to be thinking of how you would handle it. This is made even tougher due to lack of capital that most of these folks must manage. In other words, unless you are very fortunate, you won't have enough capital to just hire a good person and then address getting the work to keep him or her busy. You will have to make them billable immediately, simply because you won't have the money to pay them out of the profits you personally are generating."

"As for getting business, at least almost everyone needs your service in one way or another due to the high technology environment in which we all operate. Probably one of the best things you can do to help yourself, it seems to me, is to just tell the world you are open for business. You can do this through personal phone calls, emails, social media, and even some advertising in business journals and neighborhood newspapers. One specific thing I did when I started in the insurance business was join a referral group, or tips club, as some people called it. It was a group of sales people and small business owners that met for lunch once a week and exchanged leads. Like I said earlier, almost everyone is a potential customer for you, so you should be easy to refer to. I bet that your wife's CPA firm will turn into a lucrative source of business for you too. I also remember telling Randy about Associated Builders & Contractors, because I thought it was a natural for him. I'm not sure it is for you, but there may be some group out there that would be great for you. Have you heard of Associated Builders & Contractors?"

"Yes, I have," Randy answered. "Sharlene Ellis at Regency Bank said one of their group was a member, and that it had been a good source of business leads for him."

"I know him very well," Steve added. "He is a great banker and individual, and is well thought of in ABC. However, I think you should know that developing good relations based on respect and trust take time. I don't think you can just show up at an ABC meeting, or any trade group meeting for that matter, and expect people to start coming to you for help in their business. You probably need to be prepared to show them your sincerity and let the business evolve over time. You will need to be active on committees and projects as they come up. Since your business is very time intensive, you have to weigh the benefits of this involvement versus your need to work and generate billable time."

"Mike, I actually need to leave shortly, Steve informed Mike. Believe it or not, I have an ABC meeting I need to get to. I don't want to miss the social hour and the chance to visit with all my friends and customers that will be there. By the way, I will mention your name to my associates and customers as I get the chance to. I wish you great success with your new venture, and please get in touch if something comes up that I can help with. We all like to see an entrepreneur succeed."

Mike thanked Steve as he left the office and headed to the restaurant to work on the new installation. His thoughts were racing as he recalled his meeting and what he had learned. He was encouraged by what he had heard, and felt energized and optimistic, yet he could not stop thinking of the risk which he was in the midst of taking, along with the fear and anguish of potential failure. He still had the lingering doubt and the fact that **time was, and still is, the enemy.**

CHAPTER SIXTEEN

READY OR NOT!

"Shoot!" Randy spoke out loud as he noticed the time on his computer screen. He did not realize it was after midnight. He had become so focused on making follow up notes and looking up contact info for potential customers that he had lost track of time. Oh well, he thought. I probably could not have gone to sleep even if had gone to bed earlier, but now I am exhausted. He felt this strange anxiety that something was happening whether he was **ready or not!**

Harry Hanson had reviewed the cash projections and pointed out that Randy may not have included enough for vehicle and equipment fuel and repairs. He pointed out that Randy's figure for business property tax looked much too high. Randy immediately saw his mistake. He applied the county rate for his school district to the entire cost of equipment, instead of applying it to the assessed value, which Harry said tends to be about 10% to 12% of the actual cost. This was good news and more than offset the increased vehicle and equipment cost, which he agreed was too low, after thinking through it again. However, he also has forgot to include the cost for the CPA to prepare his statement for the bonding company. The overall net result was a slight increase in projected expenses, causing him to grimace at the thought of needing even more business.

Randy knew the following day would be a busy one. He had to contact Sharlene Ellis and he also planned to look into cashing out some of his 401(K) money. He didn't like the fact that Josh had come up with $12,000 for the equipment down-payment, and he had not come up with anything. It was better, he thought, that he just take the money from the 401(K) than to use the savings Vicky and he had, which he was disappointed to learn, was just $8,000. Harry had said it best to use savings first, but it just wasn't that much, and he didn't want to alarm Vicky with another surprise just yet.

He also had set up lunch with Paul Burnhart, the city's park director. He was in charge of all city landscaping and park maintenance. Randy thought he had a good relationship with Paul and was hoping to capitalize on that to get some work. He also needed to meet with Josh and plan the details for their first day of actual business, not to mention getting the post office box. Randy finally went to bed for a few hours of sleep before he faced another demanding day.

Sharlene Ellis's voice message informed Randy that she was out for a banking conference and would not be back until the following day. Well, that part will have to wait a while he thought, as he called Josh.

"Hi Josh, I hope you're rested up and ready to go. We are getting real close to the big day," Randy tried to be upbeat.

"Of course, I am, Randy," Josh joked. "In fact, I am ready to start right now. By the way, one of my real estate guys gave me a lead with a lady that is developing a zero-lot line housing addition. She plans to get started by the end of the year. We have a shot at the grass work and fencing. It should be a pretty good job if we can get it."

"That is awesome, Josh," Randy exclaimed with excitement. "That would be at just the right time too. I have a meeting with Paul Burnhart, the park director. Maybe things are looking up for us. I need to get the W-4 forms to you for the guys and you to complete. I may wait until I see the banker, just in case there is some paperwork for us to sign. I assume you are okay with doing our banking there. Oh by the way, please don't forget we have to pick up the equipment, probably next Tuesday."

"No problem with the equipment," Josh assured Randy. "I am also good with using your friend at Regency Bank. I don't really know any bankers anyway."

"Do you think our big customer will let us bill every two weeks instead of monthly?" Randy asked.

"I will find out for sure, but my guess is they will. They owe us one anyway, since we are giving them a discount from what they are paying now," Josh jokingly responded.

"Well then great. I will get in touch as soon as I meet with the banker, and we will go from there. Do you need me to do anything as far as getting prepared to open is concerned?" Randy inquired.

"No, nothing right now," Josh said. "We probably need to check out the equipment when it arrives and buy a couple of fuel containers, but other than that, I think we will be good to go, and I am very much ready to do it."

Randy couldn't help but appreciate Josh's calm and optimistic manner, as he noticed a call coming in from Paul Burnhart. He thought quickly that Paul may be calling to cancel lunch, but he thought Paul had sounded interested in talking when they scheduled it.

"Hi Paul, you aren't calling to cancel on me, are you?" Randy asked nervously.

"Hi Randy, not at all. I want to have lunch, but I do have to be way out north of downtown at 1:00, so I was wondering if you can meet me early, say around 11:30."

"I am happy to do that," Randy sighed with relief. "What about Brownie's Hamburger Place? That will be on your way."

"Perfect," Paul agreed.

Randy was excited. Since he had some time before lunch, he went by the maintenance office at the community college to register as a vendor for lawn and landscape services. You never know, he thought.

Randy saw a call coming in from an unknown number. He thought that he would not answer such calls in the past, but he was not about to miss any call that could possibly be related to business, so he answered.

The person calling said, "Hello, my name is Don Adams. I saw your name on Angie's list, and I am looking for someone to give me a price on lawn services and general maintenance for four commercial buildings."

Randy was astonished, "Of course I am interested, Don. How can I look at your property and give you an estimate?"

"I will just text you the addresses and you can go look at them at your convenience, but I would like to know within a week or so," Don offered.

"That is perfect. I will get back to you in a day or two," Randy promised. He was pulling into the parking lot at Brownie's and almost hit the building. He was so excited from this unexpected call that he was having some difficulty just driving. I must calm down he thought, otherwise Paul will think I am losing it. Anyway, he planned to go and price out Don Adams's work as soon as the text arrived with the addresses.

"Hi Paul, and thanks for joining me for lunch, because I know how busy you are," Randy greeted Paul as he sat down at the booth Randy had secured. After some social chatter and speculation about the upcoming city council elections, Randy became serious. "Paul, what do you think about me starting out on my own?" Randy asked candidly.

"Well, you are sure not beating around the bush any longer," Paul replied. "I, of course, believe you are talented and conscientious. At the same time, you have a lot of established competition, such as your former company. I will be more than happy to consider all your bids for city work, but you have to beat your competition for me to recommend your proposals. Of course, the lowest price doesn't always guarantee you get the contract, but it is a huge factor. I can submit your bids and see they are at least considered, and I will do that, but the bottom line is you have to put together professional and convincing proposals that are priced right. Fair enough?"

Randy was determined and intent with his reply, "Paul, I will submit proposals that impress even you, and I will do the work to perfection, if the City, and you, will just give me a chance."

"I believe my bosses will give you consideration," Paul assured Randy. "In fact, we have a couple things coming up soon that you could probably do. One is a tree planting all along I-75. The addition of a new lane each direction has been completed out there. There will also be some sod work involved. It will be at least a $50,000 job. We also will be trimming trees at all city parks within the next year, which in itself is a major project. Of course, you would need the right equipment for this one."

"Do you have any routine maintenance work that you sub out?" Randy curiously asked.

"Actually, we do hire contractors to do the mowing at the three library sites, as well as some of the parks, if you are interested in that type of work," Paul answered. "Those are all on an annual contract that renews June 30, which is the City's fiscal year-end."

"I have been told that I will have to get bonding for certain types of work," Randy stated. "Does the City require any bonding for the work you just mentioned? Or, is there any other financial requirement or commitment involved?"

"The I-75 contract will require a bond for the amount of the contract, for sure, and the tree trimming work might," Paul quickly volunteered. "We also require a minimum of a review financial statement annually, if you know what that means."

Randy laughed, "I don't really know what it means, but I have had two CPA's and an insurance agent tell me to be prepared to provide them. I take it then that the maintenance doesn't require a bond?"

"We haven't asked for a bond on that work in the past," Paul answered. "I assume this is because of the nature of the work and lack of exposure to the City if the contractor doesn't perform. I have to go now, Randy, and thank you for the lunch.

I wish you all the best and believe you have a good chance of making it work. By the way, I saw your former boss, Ted, last week. He actually didn't have anything good to say about you, so if I were you, I would expect him to be highly competitive with you. Just a heads up."

"Thank you, Paul, for taking time to talk to me and for all the info about working with the City. It means a lot to me that the City, and you, will at least give me a chance to prove what I can do," Randy expressed in a truly grateful tone. "I also appreciate the heads-up about Ted. Looks like he intends to make it as hard as he can for me to make a go of this."

Randy was now in a more sober tone than when he arrived for lunch with Paul, realizing the serious nature of dealing with the City. Checking his phone, he saw a voicemail from Sharlene Ellis and the text from Don Adams. Sharlene said she could meet in two days at 9:00 in the morning. Randy plugged the meeting into his calendar and left a message confirming it with Sharlene. He then headed to the area of town where Don's buildings were located. He was now worried about this bonding thing, thinking he should make Steve Palmer aware of what Paul had told him about the City's requirements.

"Hello, Randy," Steve answered on the first ring. "What are you up to today?"

Randy told Steve about his conversation with Paul, and asked, "How tough would it be to get a $50,000 bond?"

Steve seemed optimistic as he replied, "It will be more difficult for a start-up, but it isn't impossible. I represent one company, based in Shawnee, that works with smaller contractors and they do sometimes write bonds for contractors that haven't been in business that long. We will have to convince them of your capabilities and those of your partner. You will also have to have capital showing on your balance sheet of probably a minimum of $20,000. You will also need to show liquidity by having a current ratio of at least one to one."

"What?" was Randy's puzzled response. "I don't even know what that means, much less know whether I have it or not."

Steve was patient with Randy and offered a brief explanation. "Your capital is the difference between your assets and liabilities. These appear on your balance sheet that the CPA firm will prepare for you. Liquidity is a term financial people use to describe a company's ability to pay its bills when they come due. For example, if you owe $10,000, you would need $10,000 to pay those bills. Thus, if you have $10,000 of cash or accounts receivable equal to the bills you owe, then you have a current ratio of one to one. On the other hand, if you spent all your money for a piece of equipment and still owe $10,000 in bills, you have a very poor current ratio, which is called being illiquid. Does this seem to make sense?"

"Well, somewhat, but I think I may be in trouble already," Randy tried to explain. "Josh put $12,000 into our account, and we used it for a down payment on a lease for our equipment. I remember the equipment dealer saying it was a capital lease since we own the equipment at the end of the lease. We owe the rest of the lease which I think is about $36,000, due over three years. I am taking $12,000 from my 401(K) to put in the company account. So where do I stand?"

"Believe it or not, Randy, you may not be in as bad a financial condition as you think. If I understand what you just said, you have $12,000 of capital and a $36,000 liability. However, only one-third of the liability is a current liability, which means it is the portion of the lease that is due within one year. That is the definition of a current liability. It is one that must be paid within one year. Although you owe $36,000 on the lease, only $12,000 is due within one year. Once you put the $12,000 from your 401(K) in the company as capital, it will have $12,000 of current assets, which would be cash of course. A current asset has the same definition as a current liability, meaning it is cash already, or will be converted to cash within a year. For example, when you bill your customer, it is an account receivable. Accounts receivable are expected to be collected within a year, so they are current assets. The same would be true for inventory being held for use on jobs, assuming of course, you expect to use the inventory on a job within a year. But getting back to our situation, you will have a current ratio of one to one because the $12,000 of cash in the bank equals the $12,000 owed within the next year on the lease. You will also show $24,000 of capital, which is the money Josh and you have put in the business, Of course, you have long-term debt of $36,000, represented by the balance owed on the lease. To make your books balance, which they must always do, you also have equipment of $48,000. Since you have a capital lease, it is treated just like you borrowed the $48,000 at the bank and paid for the equipment."

After a brief pause, Steve continued, "Now back to the likelihood of securing a bond. Even though your balance sheet won't look too bad, you have no track record of making a profit. Because you have never owned a business before and can't show your ability to make a profit, the insurance company is going to be more skeptical than if you had been in business for a while. They will want more capital and liquidity in the business than they might otherwise require. That means you are probably going to have to come up with some more capital, represented by cash. I can't know for sure, but it might be as much as another $20,000 to $30,000. It will also help if you are showing some net profit at the time you are applying for the bond."

Randy had pulled into a parking lot to listen to Steve's explanation. He was very intent on understanding Steve's comments and frankly was struggling to do so. "Whew, Steve, that was quite an oratory. I may need a refresher course soon, but I think I do get the overall picture. Bottom line is that I really need to show a profit for the next few months, even if it isn't all that much, and I have to be looking for more capital that can be just sitting in cash for a rainy day. Am I even close to being right?"

Steve chuckled, "Yes, Randy, you are very close to right. You should have your accountant go over your financial statements every month for a while until you have a good concept of reading them and knowing where you stand. By the way, do you have any ideas on the capital part?"

"I am not positive, to be honest," Randy admitted. "Although, I do have some equity in my house that I might be able to use for some money to put in the company. Also, Josh's Dad is pretty well off and has told Josh he could let him use up to $50,000 if Josh and I really need it."

"Just remember, it needs to be capital, not debt," Steve cautioned. "Call me any time if I can help you on that. Your accounting firm can also be a big help as well. They also can help you make sure it is not disadvantageous for tax purposes."

"Thanks, Steve, you're the best," Randy said as he pulled out of the parking lot to look at the properties for his new prospective client. What a day this was turning out to be, he thought.

Randy spent much of the afternoon inspecting the four commercial properties and estimating the costs for maintaining them. It had the potential to be a good customer, but he needed to talk to Josh about committing to weekly recurring work. He thought they would have time to do it, but he wanted Josh to sign off on it before submitting the proposal.

"Hi Randy, Josh answered quickly. "What's up?"

Randy quickly related his day's events to Josh, and asked Josh his thoughts on the commercial building lawn care project.

"Well, first of all, way to go Bro!" Josh exclaimed. "You are definitely the man, talking to the City Park Director and then landing this other job. First thing you know we will be busy 24/7 and having to turn down work. But seriously, we can easily handle that job with the two guys we have now. Actually, since they have quite a lot of time off in December, January, and February, they don't object to working from daylight to dark the rest of the year. In fact, we can take on a lot more of that kind of work if you can get it. I also know it would be easy to get more help, even temporary help, if we needed it. I either know the people that are willing to work on that basis, or I know those that can find them for us. So, I've got your back on that, Randy. Trust me."

"Well, we don't have anything yet, but you are reassuring with your confidence as to getting the work done," Randy admitted. "What about the equipment for doing the tree planting? Are you familiar with that?"

Josh thought for a moment and answered, "Well we would have to either rent or buy a small flatbed and an auger. I don't really know what that would cost, but my guess would be at least $10,000, even for used gear."

"I kind of thought that too," Randy immediately said. "Okay, I will see what Don Adams has to say and let you know."

Randy immediately called Don Adams and gave him his proposal for the basic lawn care and maintenance of the four properties. He knew he was offering a very fair deal, but was totally taken by surprise when Don replied, "Sounds fair to me, Randy. Please plan to start next week. I guess you will bill me monthly?" Randy was too stunned to ask for bi-weekly billing and just answered, "Sure."

Randy was so excited at the turn of events of the day that he couldn't wait to get home and tell Vicky all about it. She was excited for Randy, and was relieved that Randy was beginning to see some business come in. She knew very well how much the lack of anything tangible had been worrying him in recent weeks.

Randy spent the evening updating his cash flow projection for the new business and also continuing his list of calls and contacts. He was relieved to know of the opportunity with the City and, of course, the actual new customer. There now could be no doubt about the reality of his business venture. It was unfolding before his very eyes and he realized that things were now happening whether he was **ready or not**, and he had better get ready.

CHAPTER SEVENTEEN

CHILLING FACTS

Randy woke up before his alarm went off at 6:00. He had purposely set the alarm early because he did not want to slip into a bad habit of sleeping late. His instinct was telling him to be prepared to get up early and stay up late. The **chilling facts** of all that would be required of him to make this business a success began rolling through his mind, particularly the capital requirement issues mentioned first by Harry, and now by Paul Burnhart and Steve Palmer. He decided to quickly dress and get out of the house before he woke up Vicky. A good cup of hot coffee from Java Don's sounded good anyway. Besides, he wanted to ask Norm, the manager, if any of his friends were interested in doing business with him.

"Well my goodness, look who just walked through the door! Long time, no see, Randy," Norm blasted out as he saw Randy.

"I know, Norm, but I have been really busy the past couple weeks," Randy replied half apologetically. Randy ordered his usual, and shared with Norm briefly where he was on starting the business. "Have any of your friends or customers shown any interest in doing business with me?" Randy asked inquisitively.

Norm seemed pleased and a little excited to inform Randy, "Of course my friend. In fact, I was going to call you today, because I have five business cards from customers that say they would not mind talking to you. Some of these people are in the real estate business, either construction or agents. One or two work for big companies here in town. This one lady, I do know for sure, seemed real interested. She is property manager for, I guess, a big management company of some sort. So here they are, and good luck. You need to come by more often because that would motivate me to find more business for you."

Randy was virtually speechless. He did remember Norm saying he would try to drum up some business, but he had no faint idea it would amount to this. "Norm, I don't even know what to say, or how to thank you, but thank you so much. Maybe I can do you a favor sometime."

"Well, you could come in more often and drink more coffee, but you don't owe me anything. I am happy that I could help you. In fact, I actually am excited that I can be a little part of what you are doing."

Randy visited with Norm for almost an hour, learning what he could about the five leads Norm had given him. He was bursting with excitement and anticipation at what adventures he might encounter with these people. He came back down to earth and thought it might be good to call Travis and get a feel for what the tree planting equipment might cost, and while he was at it, perhaps check out the tree trimming equipment.

"Hi Travis, hope you are doing well. I am trying to check out the equipment, and its cost of course, that I would need to plant trees as well as to trim and dispose of tree limbs. Do you deal in that?"

"Hello, Randy, it is nice to hear from you. First of all, don't forget that your equipment will arrive tomorrow. You can pick it up as soon as the bank will release your cashiers' check. To answer your question, yes, I can get that type of equipment, but it is hard to say what it will cost. There is such a large range of sizes, types, and quality that it could range all over the place. One thing I don't deal in that you will need is a bucket, and those can be pretty pricey. If you would like, I can look up a name and number of someone that might help you with that. Otherwise, sure, I will do some checking and let you know the costs. But, I must tell you, the lessor I got for you on your equipment is not likely to do any more until you have a track record. I don't mind asking, but I have done business with them for years, and sort of know their thinking."

"No rush, Travis, but as you can work it in, I would like to learn more about this equipment," Randy replied. "I don't even have the job I would need it for, but I do know the opportunity is coming later on this year."

"Good morning, Randy, I am so pleased to meet you. I am Sharlene Ellis, but please call me Shari." Randy was immediately impressed with the professional demeanor and pleasant personality of the banker he had known only as Freddy's daughter-in-law until now.

"Good morning to you, Shari, and thank you for seeing me," Randy offered. "Your Dad is one of my favorite people, and I have known him forever."

"Well thank you very much, and he has told me a little about you," Shari continued. "But please tell me what you are trying to do."

Randy spent fifteen minutes recounting his experiences of the past couple months, and concluded by saying, "I am not sure what you can do to help me, but would like to know if you can."

Shari thought for a moment, and began her reply, "Randy, let me begin by saying that I admire you for the hard work you are doing. I enjoy working with entrepreneurs and small business owners very much. I also congratulate you on the planning you have already done. I could count on one hand the number of start-up individuals I have met that had done a cash flow projection before they came to talk to me. In fact, not many more than that even knew what one was. Even though you give credit for that to someone else, you still had to do the work to come up with the numbers and put them all together, so congratulations to you."

"Unfortunately," Shari continued after a brief pause, "Our bank, or any bank for that matter, must work within a tight framework in our lending practices. The government regulators are quite stringent with us. Any loan they feel is not of prime quality can be categorized by them in such a manner that our bank must have capital to cover it. It is like they won't let us show it as an asset. They particularly are critical of loans to start-ups and loans that aren't properly secured by what we call collateral. Collateral serves as a back-up for repayment of the loan if our customer is not able to pay it back from cash flow. Depending on the type of collateral, we may or may not be able to get comfortable with it and may have to get additional collateral on top of the asset being purchased with the loan."

"We have to evaluate each loan from the viewpoint of what we call the three C's. These are character, capacity, and collateral. First, we have to determine our customer, the borrower, is of good character. Naturally, we don't want to do business with someone who is of poor character, because they might not really try to pay us back, particularly if the situation turned sour, second is capacity, which is the ability to repay the loan. In other words, does the borrower have the proven, consistent cash flow to make the payments on the loan? Last is the collateral, which I have mentioned, and it is last because it may be the least important. As you can probably surmise by now, we really must lend only to people of good character, who want and intend, to pay the loan; and, who have a somewhat proven background of being able to do so. The collateral is only to provide a margin of safety, but believe me, no banker wants to rely on the collateral alone, unless maybe it is of such guaranteed value that it clearly could more than cover the amount of the loan."

"Even though I don't like to discourage you, and wish you all the best, many times my hands are somewhat tied as far as making the loan is concerned. While, your character may be impeccable, if your cash flow is marginal, or if the collateral is of questionable resale value, we still would not be able to lend to you, and not because we don't want to. Lending is our business and the source of much of our revenue, so of course, we want to make loans."

"With all that being said, there are, at times, things we can do to get a loan done. For example, you might pledge a second mortgage on your home, or you might know a person of substantial wealth to be a guarantor on your loan."

Shari concluded, "Of course, we would like to do your checking account business and possibly be your credit card servicer, if you need that. We offer online banking, bill pay, and remote deposit. As you grow and demonstrate profitability, we could then be in a position to do equipment financing and even a line of credit to smooth out your slow times of year, which I assume to be the winter months. For example, we could lend to you during the winter months and you would repay the line of credit down to zero during your peak season, and repeat the process each year as long as you needed that assistance."

"How long do you think it might be before we could earn this type of lending?" Randy anxiously asked.

"I couldn't give a precise answer," Shari replied, "because it varies so much depending on the size of the loan versus the profitability. It could be a year, or it could be even longer. I will say our bank tries very hard to be accommodating to small business owners and serve their needs as soon as we possibly can. But let me ask you what you have in mind?"

Randy was unsure how to respond, but did manage to organize his thoughts enough to say, "I was hoping you might lend us enough to make it through the winter months if we need it. We have to be able to make it on our own during our prime time, but as my cash flow projection shows, we may run in the red, especially during January and February. Also, if we do get some of the City's work, we will need to buy more equipment."

"I don't think it entirely impossible we could do that, Shari volunteered. "I sure can't make any promises, but if your profit and loss up through next December reflects good profitability and cash flow, and you have not added more debt than your existing equipment capital lease, it could just be possible, especially if the deficit isn't too large.

As for any new equipment, it would again depend on your results through the time you requested the loan. We can also consider the additional revenue generated by the equipment if it can be reasonably determined."

Randy seemed hopeful and thanked Shari for her time. "I understand you gave my friend, Mike, some advice when he came to see you. He told me what you said to him, but I am curious if you have any special advice for me?"

"Of course," Shari promised. "The nature of your industry makes your business more speculative than some, subject to rapid changes, turnover of customers, and non-recurring work, not to speak of swings in the economy. Because of this, I think it is extremely important you be conservative in your spending in order to accumulate capital that will allow you to make it through the inevitable tough times. A second point that I also made to your friend Mike is obtaining repetitive work. In your case, this might be a year-round customer for lawn care or about anything that can be done all the time and which will generate steady cash flow. It preferably will be something that isn't directly impacted by a slow economy. In other words, the customer has no choice but to have it done. Does that make sense to you, Randy?"

"It actually does," Randy quickly answered. "I can think of a couple things I might do along those lines. Thank you for bringing that thought to the surface. I also hear you telling me I should really hold my spending down until I am well capitalized, because a rainy day will come at some point."

"That is the main focus of my comment, Randy," Shari agreed. "We all are going to encounter our slumps in business, often times losing money for a while before we can regroup and get back to profitability. Often this might mean just surviving until the economy turns around. Oh by the way, I think you would be a natural for one of the construction contractor organizations here in town. I mentioned Associated Builders & Contractors to Mike, but another one is Associated General Contractors. Both would put you in contact with people that could refer business to you. Unlike Mike, who could be an associate member, you would have to be a regular member, and that costs more money. However, it could be money well spent. I encourage you to at least check them out. If you like, I can email you some contact info for them."

"Yes please," Randy said, "and thank you so much for all the information and advice. I really appreciate your time. I am ready to open our checking account now and did think to bring our Articles of Organization and federal identification number. I will have to take the signature cards for my partner to sign. Should I make another appointment to get that done?"

"Not at all," Shari laughed. "Let's just do it right now. I will introduce you to one of our new accounts people, and you can be done with it in thirty minutes at the most. Also, if you want, you could send me prior year tax returns and a personal financial statement for your partner and you. I can also keep a copy of your cash flow projections. With this information, I can start a file for you that will speed things along for the time you do need to make a loan request. It is possible we could do something based on the equity in your house, or just refer you to a mortgage lender we know for a refinance of your residence. That could perhaps be better than a loan against your equity by our bank. In any event, I wish you all the very best, and offer to help with anything I can. Please contact me any time if you think I can help."

"Thanks so much, Shari," Randy humbly said. "You have already helped me a lot, and I look forward to doing business with you. Also, I will have to say your Dad was absolutely right about you. You know a lot about this small business stuff."

Randy tried to organize his thoughts of the last two days as he drove home to make calls to Norm's referrals. It had been a whirlwind, and he was filled with enthusiasm and excitement… and **chilling facts.**

CHAPTER EIGHTEEN

SIXTY DAYS LATER

"Hi Mike," Tim smiled as he strolled into Mike's office. "I was hoping you have time to talk about our future relationship. I know we are both aware the big project for the County will soon be completed."

"Yes, Tim," I am glad you came in to discuss that, as I am aware it is quickly coming to its conclusion, and I am concerned as to where we go from here."

"I have been thinking about that also," Tim replied. "And I have a proposal for you. I have been handling all the emergency service calls for my ten or so largest customers. These are usually some of the more complicated requests I get, and they also seem to occur at the weirdest times. Often, I am already deeply involved with another client and these calls just add to my already tight schedule. Our business continues to grow, and I have three new installations and/or large upgrades starting soon, two of which are out-of-town, so I will be traveling quite a bit starting next week. I was able to hire a young man who should grow into a good tech, so I won't need you on a full-time basis any longer, but I need someone to handle the technical issues while I am traveling and just otherwise committed when in town. You could be the perfect fit for that, because I know you have the technical capability to handle them. I can afford to pay $100 per hour, which I know is a little under the billing rate you would like, but it would be a good steady source of income for you. These should easily add up to fifteen hours a month, and maybe more. Of course, you will have to be available most any time to field the calls. What do you think?"

"And for how long a time do you expect it will last, Tim?" Randy questioned.

"I actually would view this as almost permanent," Tim quickly replied. "At least for the foreseeable future, and for as long as you have the time. Again, all you have to agree to is that you would not attempt to divert these clients away from my business. As a further enticement, I have three more clients I am willing to transfer over to you. They will be at least twice as much in monthly billing as the first two I gave you. What do you say?"

Mike's thoughts were racing as he sat in silence. He had always held Tim in high esteem, but this offer was just over the top. "Well, Tim, you are kind to make this offer to me. I am still way short of having the work I need to make my business work, and so of course, I am interested. I do have a couple questions though, and they are when does this deal start, and how much of the trouble-shooting work is during evenings and weekends?"

Mike responded, "It is a two-way street, Mike, because you have done a lot to help build my business, and I appreciate that more than you probably know. You would continue to help me a lot with the special project work. You deserve a break as well, so I am happy to transfer the three clients to you. They will actually get better service from you I am sure and they are all long-time clients that started with me. So, I want them to be well taken care of. Anyway, I think it will be a win-win-win for all of us. The special work, as I said, will hit almost any time of the day or night. I recall about 40% has to be done after hours. But also, some of the work during regular business hours is critical, which means you would have to drop what you are doing and go do it. As for the start time, how about right now? I will call the three clients within the next two hours and give them your contact info. I will also contact you myself as the special calls arrive and give you details on where, when, who, and what to do. Fair enough?"

"Fair enough," Mike agreed.

"Thanks, Mike."

Mike sat back in his chair, trying to organize his thoughts. He drifted back in time, several months prior. He vividly recalled the confusion encountered just learning about the types of business entities, and the first meeting with Harry Hanson that resolved the issue for him, as well as Randy. He reflected on the fear, doubt, and anxiety he had experienced as he realized how little business he had and how much he appreciated that Harry had literally forced him to do a cash flow projection and think about cash needs. While it scared him to no end, at least it showed him what he was facing and thus have at least a fighting chance of making his business work. He realized he could not have made it without the valuable input from Harry. Harry had told them that being scared was a healthy thing for a business owner because it keeps one on their toes. It turned out Harry was right. Because he had been frightened out of his wits, he had learned to aggressively solicit work. He was now getting leads from friends and family. Morton & Co. had already put him in touch with two of their clients. Steve Palmer had also given him referrals to builders and developers, a couple of which had expressed some interest. He had even received inquiries from his Facebook page and website. He shuddered at the thought of where he would have been had he not come to grips with how crucial the marketing aspects were. He also credited Harry for forcing him to commit 100% to the new business, which he now realized was the divining moment he crossed the line and really committed to doing it. Had Harry not confronted him about his lack of commitment, he probably would have not done it at all and would have never known if he could really do it or not.

And then there was Heather, who agreed to return to work part-time to help with the personal budget. Again, he could not have done it without that help.

And what about Liz, his old college friend that he had not stayed in touch with that much who referred Randy and he to Harry Hanson and Ruthie for the first project at her restaurant. Not only that, Liz was letting him handle a big upgrade for her construction company that hopefully would hit in a few months. He had just wrapped up the installation for Ruthie, and it was working well for her. He was now servicing her IT needs on a monthly basis. Not only that, Ruthie had introduced him to several of her friends in the restaurant business for possible IT services. One of them agreed to a monthly service arrangement.

There was also Freddy Simon, who set Randy and he straight on the hard and cold facts of capital for new business start-ups and referred them to his daughter-in-law, Shari Ellis, the President of Regency Bank. Shari was working with him to evaluate financing options, which in all likelihood he would soon need. Shari had encouraged him to develop recurring work to provide a steady cash flow, and he was definitely taking her advice, having signed up three clients for monthly IT maintenance services.

And last, but not least, was his former boss, Tim, with whom he had just made a deal that would generate a nice amount of revenue. He was learning now what a nice person Tim actually was. He was one of those "one-in-a-lifetime" individuals you are favored to know. Who knew that Tim would react the way he did and how he would actually play a key role in helping him gather business. Who knows what his friendship with Tim would lead to in the future?

It dawned on him that he had received so much help and encouragement from so many people. He suddenly realized he was indebted to these people, all of whom had spent time and resources to selflessly help him accomplish what he could not have even begun to have done himself.

Mike quickly accessed his cash flow projection worksheet in his Dropbox account and added the estimated revenues to it. He thought how foreign this had been to him when he first started it, but how Heather had since helped him analyze, and eventually, to even understand it. She had also taught him how to set up his business in QuickBooks. He could now enter his checks and credit card charges. He had also learned to prepare his bills in QuickBooks and print his monthly financial statements. He compared them in minute detail to his cash flow projection every month and updated the projection with new revenue, and also for expenses he had not budgeted or had not budgeted for the proper amounts.

He could see that his deficit was now much narrower than it had been when he arrived at work this morning. While he remained concerned about the deficit, he now felt more determined and confident than ever he would soon close the gap entirely. He just needed a few of the new leads to pan out, and he would be there. He felt his momentum was finally beginning to really move, but also realized he would never be able to really relax entirely. He now was up to this challenge.

And then the phone rang. It was Tim. "Hi Mike. I just wanted to call the first time one of those special service calls came in. I will probably just email or text you in the future, but you need to go to WP Engineering at 211 West 7th Street. You will work with Janelle Ballard. Their main server is down and has brought work at their forty-person staff to a standstill. Can you go their right away?"

"Yes sir, I am on my way now, and thanks for everything!"

CHAPTER NINETEEN

SIX MONTHS LATER

Randy sat at his kitchen table. It had been a beautiful fall Saturday, but the rain had started in mid-afternoon, ending his work on the nice project for a new customer that was developing a small patio-home development in Clarenton, a town just thirty miles away. He was using this unexpected time to work on his most immediate issue, that of getting a bond commitment in order to bid on the I-75 project for the City. Paul Burnhart had encouraged him to bid on the job, as one of the major competitors had declined to participate due to the retirement of the owner. This was turning into a major problem for Randy. Steve Palmer had made it clear that more capital would be required in order to get the bond. He had picked up his financial statements from Heather the day before. They looked pretty good, he thought, considering the business had been up and running only about six months. The profit & loss showed about $20,000 of profit, and that was after Josh and he had taken $7,500 of salary each. It could have been better but his old boss, Ted, had really been making a point of competing hard on every project that had come up at the city. Randy had to reduce his price for several jobs in order to get the work, so his margins had been less than normal and expected. He was thinking about asking Ted for a meeting to see if Ted's relentless pressure could be alleviated, but Randy didn't expect any relief. He was determined to succeed in spite of the competition from Ted. This situation was causing his profit on contract jobs to be under industry expectations and thus causing the bonding company to be suspect of bonding for the huge city job on I-75.

On the other hand, the service work, including Josh's two major original customers was looking nice, as reflected by the P & L. His contact, Don Adams, had turned out to be a great referral source, having sent him two additional customers, both of which were even larger than that of Don. Steve Palmer had also sent him a nice recurring client. Heather had also helped him with a couple prospects that had worked out.

Steve had already told Randy he thought he would need $25,000 more capital in the business in order to secure the bond. This was on top of the equipment that would then be needed. Travis thought that would run at least $35,000. Travis still wasn't sure he could obtain a lessor for this, but now was more optimistic than he had originally been. Shari Ellis had recommended Randy refinance his house rather than secure a line-of credit at the bank. He had even applied and been approved for a mortgage, which had been difficult due to his new business and lack of verifiable guaranteed income. Thankfully, the mortgage company that Shari referred him to dealt a lot with small business owners, so he was finally approved. He would be able to net about $35,000 on the refinance. He had been thinking that he could use $25,000 of the loan proceeds for capital that Steve had said would be needed. Josh was willing to pull $25,000 from his 401(k) that could be used for most of the equipment – if they got the job. He was just hoping that Regency Bank would provide the additional $10,000 or so for the balance of the equipment. If not, he would have no choice but use the remaining $10,000 from the house financing, which he desperately wanted to hang on to, for the inevitable drop in revenues that would be facing him shortly. Like a hurricane forming at sea, it was calm and pleasant now, but just a matter of time before the winter months would be upon him. Randy tried to turn his thoughts to other issues.

It had been an exciting and sometimes frightening six months. The only thing stable about it had been Josh and the work for their original two customers. Josh had executed this work without a hitch and had also used his assistants to handle all the yard maintenance work that Randy had secured, which had added up to quite a lot, and the good news was it was continuing to grow. He also had a good backlog of special projects such as tree trimming and removal, French drains, fence repair and replacement, and others. In fact, they had been using a third part-time employee to handle this work. They had also confirmed at least one nice project from the developer that Josh's customers had referred them to. Actually, they had recently started receiving calls from not only yard maintenance customers, but also commercial contractors, including two general contractors that Steve Palmer had referred him to. Randy smiled as he recalled that Paul Burnhart at the City had done exactly what he said he would do and had seen to it that Randy at least got a chance on all the work for the City. He had obtained probably 30% of the projects he had quoted on; however, Ted's constant pressure had taken a toll on the profits from this work. He was pleased that all the projects had been completed on time and were of high quality. So, he was pleased with the growth in customers and the reputation his Company was accruing. In fact, First Lawn and Landscape, Inc. was actually becoming fairly well known around town.

He remembered an off-the-cuff comment that Heather had made to him just last week. "Randy, if you keep growing like this, you will have to get a full-time bookkeeper to do your accounting." That comment had overwhelmed him, because that would also mean an office would have to be rented, furniture and computers would have to be purchased, and a whole new list of monthly overheads would have to be paid each month. He was grateful to Heather for all she had taught him about accounting. Without her, he would never have been able to understand job accounting and have financial statements that Steve Palmer could use and show to the bonding companies. At the same time, he could see his monthly fees to Morton & Co. were increasing every month and that it was inevitable at some point, it would no longer make sense for them to the accounting.

Randy thought the time had flown by so quickly since Mike and he first drove over to Fayetteville to meet with Harry Hanson and all the confusion about the type of entity they should elect was so easily resolved by Harry. Harry was also the sole reason Mike and he had learned to think about cash flow and preparing a cash flow statement. Yes indeed, Harry probably deserved much of the credit for Randy being as far along as he was. Like Harry had predicted, Randy had remained scared of failure each and every day. Freddy Simon also had helped him a lot with his frank advice about getting the money for the business and had even got him a meeting with Shari Ellis, president of Regency Bank. Freddy likewise deserved a big high-five for that. Heather and Morton & Co. had also given him some leads and some of them had proven to be productive. No doubt that Travis had saved his bacon on the equipment by buying it from the dealer in Georgia before Randy even had the money for the down-payment. Even Ted, his former boss, had helped him with his angry reaction when he left Ted's employment and competing with him so relentlessly. Ted had sure knocked him into reality and forced him to work even harder and tougher. It had paid off.

Randy did not know how he would be able to return the favors to all the people who had helped him. He knew he had been fortunate. He had seen and heard of more than one in his industry that had failed in business. He now knew why that would not be difficult to do.

But he was now distracted by an email from Josh, saying that something had come up while he had been at the developer's office earlier that day. It was something about doing a much larger part of their project, but they would have to meet with them later in the year to discuss it more, so nothing was urgent at this time. Randy could not imagine what this might be, but decided to let it slide for now. His top priorities were the closing on his refinance, securing the bond, and hopefully getting the I-75 job, one that would stretch through the winter months.

"Randy, you said we could go to the movie, and it starts in twenty minutes," Vicky startled Randy as she walked into the kitchen. "Vicky, you are absolutely right, and one thing I have learned in the past six months is that I had better do what I said I would do."

www.ingramcontent.com/pod-product-compliance
Lightning Source LLC
LaVergne TN
LVHW012035230125
801952LV00001B/105
* 9 7 8 1 9 4 3 1 2 7 6 9 6 *